JAPANESE COOKING
with kids

Debra Samuels • Mayumi Uejima-Carr

Food Photography and Styling by Yumi Komatsudaira

Kid Photos by Jacob Dylan Villaruz and Darwin Villaruz

TUTTLE Publishing
Tokyo | Rutland, Vermont | Singapore

Contents

Yokoso! Welcome!	4
A Message from the TABLE FOR TWO Kids President	5
A Note to the Adults in the Room	6
Important Elements of Japanese Cuisine	8
Let's Eat More Healthy Food!	12
Basic Japanese Ingredients	14
Equipment	18
Count to Ten in Japanese While Cleaning All Parts of Your Hands!	20
Basic Cooking Techniques	21

CHAPTER 1
Japanese Rice

Let's Make Japanese Rice	26
Tuna Mayo Rice Balls	28
Kawaii Rice Balls	30
Crispy Soy Sauce Glazed Rice Balls	33
Rice Sandwiches	34
Chicken and Egg Rice Bowls	36

CHAPTER 2
Flavors from the Sea

Make Your Own Chopstick Rests	40
Dashi Soup Stock	42
Simple Nori Furikake—Tasty Seaweed Rice Sprinkles	43
Furikake Popcorn	44
Nori Jam	45
Salmon and Vegetables in Miso Sauce	46
Teriyaki Salmon Bowls	48
Tuna and Cucumber Sushi Rolls	50
Wakame, Cucumber and Cherry Tomato Salad	52
Japanese-style Tuna Pasta	53

CHAPTER 3
Food from Soy

Chopsticks Challenge!	56
Crunchy Edamame Rolls	57
Rice-stuffed Tofu Pockets (Inari Sushi)	58
Miso Dip with Vegetables	59
Teriyaki Sauce	60
Miso Soup with Vegetables	61
Tofu Croquettes	62

CHAPTER 4
Vegetables & Fruit

Mottainai (What a Waste!)	66
Green Veggies with Sesame Dressing	67
Grape Tomato Hearts	68
Clementine Juice Jelly Cups	69
Edible Decorations for Your Plate	70
Japanese Vegetable Fried Rice	72
Carrot Ginger Dressing	73
Fruit Sandos	74

CHAPTER 5
Japanese Favorites

Okosama Lunch—Kid's Lunch Special	78
Learn How to Read a Nutrition Label	81
Ramen	82
Miso Ramen	84
Ramen Eggs—Soy Sauce Seasoned Boiled Eggs	86
Kid's Special Stir-fried Udon Noodles	87
Japanese Savory Pancakes	88
Pot Stickers	90
Teddy Bear Chicken and Veggie Omurice	92

CHAPTER 6
School Lunches

Kyushoku—Japanese School Lunches	96

CHAPTER 7
Bento Box Lunch

List Foods of Each Color	98
Kawaii Bento	100
Quick Lemony Cucumber Pickles	102
Octopus-shaped Hot Dogs	103
JFC! Japanese Fried Chicken	104
Rice with Tricolored Toppings	106
Super Spiral Sando	108
Rolled Omelet	110

CHAPTER 8
Desserts & Drinks

Sugar Detective!	112
Sweet Pancake Sandwiches with Azuki Bean Jam and Strawberries	114
Japanese Matcha Tea Cake with Chocolate Swirls	116
Japanese Fruit Parfait with Mochi Balls and Ice Cream	118
Sweet and Salty Glazed Mochi Balls	120
Matcha Latte	122
Japanese Roasted Barley Tea	123
Strawberry Soy Milk	123

Resources	124
Index	124
Acknowledgments	127
A Note About the Photos	127

Yokoso! Welcome!

Hi kids, this is Debra and Mayumi, the authors of this cookbook. This book is based on our successful Japanese cooking program "Wa-Sho: Learn. Cook. Eat Japanese!," which thousands of kids just like you have attended!

With this book in hand, you're headed on an exciting journey! These recipes have gotten "two thumbs up" over and over again.

In these pages, you'll find recipes like sushi rolls and *miso* soup—which you may have tried already—plus other Japanese favorites like mochi, *onigiri* and *okonomiyaki* to make for your family.

Each chapter has fun, hands-on activities that we know you'll enjoy—like growing your own green onions or making your own chopstick rests!

Be on the lookout in the photos for traditional Japanese cloths used for wrapping *bento* boxes, wiping counters and as bandanas when cooking, and for cute

Top Author Debra Samuels
Right Author Mayumi Uejima-Carr

Because the recipes call for using knives and a stove, always ask an adult if they should join you in the kitchen before you prepare any of these dishes.

(*kawaii*) knick-knacks, chopstick rests and toys!

With a parent's permission, please e-mail photos of the foods you make to us at wa-shokuiku@tablefor2.org.

Enjoy cooking and eating our delicious (*oishii*) recipes and learning about Japanese food!

Issho ni ganbarimashou!
Let's do our best together!

Debra and Mayumi

A Message from the TABLE FOR TWO Kids President

Hi! It's Ria, the TABLE FOR TWO Kids President. I'm 14 years old, and I have been helping with Wa-Sho (short for *Wa-Shokuiku*—"Japanese food education") classes since I was 7! During my time here, I have seen that it isn't just us kids who enjoy Wa-Sho—it's the adults too! Wa-Sho has helped kids who don't eat healthy foods, or are picky eaters to recognize how fun and tasty food can be! I hope this book teaches you what it taught me—that nutritious food tastes amazing, and it's even more fun when made with family and friends!

Ria

A Note to the Adults in the Room

We are Mayumi Uejima-Carr, the President of **TABLE FOR TWO USA**, and Debra Samuels, cookbook author, food educator and Japanese food specialist. We are part of a nonprofit organization originally from Japan that addresses hunger and health issues across the globe.

In Japan, food education is an element of "whole-child development" known as *shokuiku* (food education). We were inspired by these programs to create a similar food education program for American students. To that end, we gathered a team of experts to help us achieve this goal, and the innovative Japanese-inspired food education program called "*Wa-Shokuiku*: Learn. Cook. Eat Japanese!" was born. This program, called "Wa-Sho" for short, is the foundation of this book, which teaches the importance of good nutrition in nourishing young minds and bodies.

These programs have been enthusiastically received by students, teachers, administrators and parents, and the number of students we are serving has skyrocketed. Wa-Sho is welcome in home kitchens, where parents and children can learn together. To date, the program has reached more than 23,000 people in schools and community

Above Debra demonstrates how to make *bento* to students in Boston.

Above center Kid's *bento* with *kawaii onigiri*, egg omelet and mini hot dog octopuses.
Above right Making a sushi roll!

organizations across the United States. We want to bring the Wa-Sho program to as many students as possible. Your book purchase will help to provide our food education program to more children.

Students and parents report that the classes make them more conscious of nutrition, help them develop cooking skills, increase their awareness of social issues such as food waste and teach them about Japanese culture.

Children are more interested in trying new foods if they are involved in the preparation. Wa-Sho also provides kids with an opportunity to expand their interest in food, and be more conscious of what they eat.

We are delighted to share the recipes that our instructors have taught to thousands of kids. To facilitate a child's experience and ensure their safety, some adult supervision is advisable for the recipes requiring the use of sharp implements and cooking on the stove. **We urge you to review each recipe beforehand to determine the level of assistance needed.** We look forward to hearing your wonderful stories!

Above Kids are curious about how to make *miso* soup.

Above center Mayumi with students taking the Wa-Sho program.
Above right Students making heart-shaped tomatoes!

Important Elements of Japanese Cuisine

Japanese cuisine is not just about the food and ingredients that make it Japanese; there are concepts in presentation and practice that contribute as well. The following are some of the main principles we teach in our classes.

Create Variety and Balance in Your Meals

Japanese meals have a wide variety of foods that are served in small portions on individual plates with about an equal serving size. You still feel satisfied when you have a balanced meal.

Itadakimasu & Gochisosama
Expressions of gratitude

At the beginning of a meal, you say *itadakimasu* meaning, "I receive (with respect)." You show gratitude to the source of the food—harvested animals and plants—as well as to all the people who were involved in preparing the food. At the end of a meal, you say *gochisosama*. This is also acknowledgment and gratitude to the people who helped bring the food to your plate.

Me de Taberu
The art of presentation

Me de Taberu literally means to "eat with your eyes." That means you "taste" or enjoy food first by sight, before tasting with your mouth. In Japanese dishes, presentation is important for making food look appetizing and enjoyable!

Hara Hachibu
Eat until you are 80% full

Hara hachibu is a Japanese saying that means "eat until you are 80% full." Don't stuff yourself! Sometimes we take more than we should eat and end up feeling like we might burst! If you eat just until you feel satisfied, you will help your body keep a healthy weight.

Mottainai *What a waste!*

Mottainai is usually translated as "what a waste." It is an ancient Buddhist term from Japan that means to have respect for the resources around you, to not waste resources and to use them with a sense of gratitude.

Kazoku Danran
Eating a meal together is good for your health!

Kazoku means "family," and *danran* essentially means "spending good time together." When we eat with family and friends there is a warm feeling of togetherness. We enjoy our food more, encourage each other and have conversations.

Using the Five Colors
Make your meals colorful!

The presence of different colors is an important consideration when planning a Japanese meal. From a *bento* box for a kindergartner to a traditional multi-course meal at an elegant restaurant, the person who prepares the meal has color combinations in mind. Aside from looking appetizing, a variety of colorful foods also can provide a range of nutrients. If you want to create a healthy meal, make it colorful! Red, black, green, yellow and white are the important colors in Japanese meals. Red could be a tomato or meat. Green could be broccoli or cabbage. Yellow—an orange or a sweet potato. White—tofu or rice. Black—seaweed or mushrooms.

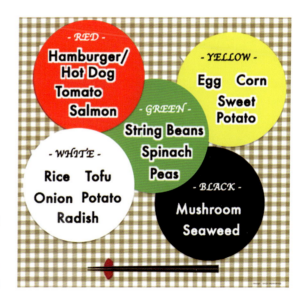

Eat Seasonal Foods

Food tastes best when it is "in season," meaning that it's ready to be harvested. This is the time of peak flavor, when the nutrients are most concentrated. Seasonality usually refers to vegetables and fruit, but it can also apply to fish and meat. For instance, mackerel are in season in autumn, fiddlehead ferns in spring and watermelon in summer!

Let's Eat More Healthy Food!

Go! Grow! Glow!* is a concept to help explain how food we eat affects our bodies. We use this idea when we teach about the nutrition in the food we are cooking. Food helps you to get energy, grow and fight diseases to stay healthy. It is also important to be aware of not only what you are eating, but how much you eat to maintain a weight that is right for you. The amounts given below are guidelines. Sometimes you may eat more, sometimes less. With this information, you can start to make your own wise choices.

GO — CARBOHYDRATES

Rice, Bread and Pasta

You need energy to walk, run, play and learn—just about any activity. Just like cars need gas to move, your body needs food to help you carry out your daily tasks and regulate your body processes.

RIGHT AMOUNT: BE CAREFUL WITH CARBS! Too many could cause health issues. Make a Fist! **The size of your fist per meal** is just about the right serving size.

GROW — PROTEINS

Meat, Fish, Soy, Dairy, Nuts, Beans and Eggs

Your body needs to build new cells and tissue such as bone, teeth, skin and muscle for growth. Babies and young children use nutrients to grow quickly. Adults use these nutrients to maintain their bodies and for strength.

RIGHT AMOUNT: OPEN YOUR HAND! The standard serving size for any variety of high protein food is roughly **the size of your palm per meal**.

---

* The concept "Go! Grow! Glow!" was developed by the US Department of Agriculture, Food and Consumer Service. Adapted from U.S. Department of Agriculture, Team Nutrition. USDA does not endorse any products, services or organizations. Provided by TABLE FOR TWO.

> **A well-balanced diet helps you to GO! GROW! GLOW!**
>
> When you are healthy and happy, you **"GLOW!"**

GLOW

FRUITS AND VEGETABLES

Broccoli, Peas, Seaweed, Carrots, Cabbage, Green Beans, Corn, Strawberries, Watermelon... The List is Endless!

Fruits, vegetables and sea vegetables like seaweed have vitamins and nutrients that fight infections, help your body repair itself when you are sick and help you stay healthy.

> **RIGHT AMOUNT:** CUP YOUR HANDS TOGETHER! That's right! You need about **two cupped handfuls of veggies and fruits per day.**

Basic Japanese Ingredients

Japanese food has become so popular worldwide that the standard ingredients may already be in your pantry! There are several condiments and seasonings associated with Japanese cooking that we use in this cookbook. Many of these ingredients are available at well-stocked supermarkets and all are available online.

❶ Kewpie Mayonnaise This Japanese brand of mayonnaise is a spread made with egg yolks and a special blend of vinegar, oil and seasonings. The bottle is hiding a secret—a second applicator! Flip the red top open and you see a circular opening. Unscrew the cap to reveal a star-shaped opening.

❷ Okonomiyaki Sauce This sauce is thick and brown and has a vinegary taste. It is made with tomatoes, fruit, vinegar and spices, and it comes in a convenient package. We use this sauce on *okonomiyaki* pancakes and in stir-fried *udon* noodles (*yaki udon*). If you can't find it in a store, there's a recipe to make your own on page 89.

❸ Mirin This thick, syrupy liquid is made by adding sweeteners to a very-low-alcohol rice wine. It adds sweetness and a shiny glaze to foods. Check with an adult before using.

❹ Soy Sauce Soy sauce (*shoyu*) is the most popular of Asian seasonings. You probably have some in your fridge or pantry! It is a brown liquid made from combining crushed soybeans, salt, wheat and a healthy mold that helps it ferment. Soy sauce can help *preserve* (keep safe) food as well as add flavor.

❺ Tamari Soy Sauce *Tamari* is a gluten-free soy sauce that is mixed with crushed soybeans, salt, rice and a healthy mold. Substitute this for regular soy sauce in any recipe.

❻ Rice Vinegar This vinegar is made by fermenting rice, which gives it a mildly sour taste. It is not as strong as regular white vinegar, which is made with fermented fruit. It is used to season sushi rice and make salad dressings. Read the label carefully—SEASONED rice vinegar includes added sugar and salt.

❼ Miso This salty ingredient is fermented soybean paste, and it is used to make the oh-so popular *miso* soup! It also makes a delicious addition to sauces and dips for vegetables. There is *shiro* (white) *miso*—the mildest and least salty, *aka* (red) *miso*—the darkest and most salty, and *awase miso* (a mixture of both red and white). Some *miso* contains *dashi* fish stock.

❽ Matcha This ingredient is powdered green tea leaves. It has a beautiful bright green color. It does contain caffeine, so check with an adult before using. You can use it to make a drink or for baking. There is also matcha that is specifically formulated for baking. We use regular matcha but you can use either kind. Be careful—many matcha brands now contain sugar. Use sugar-free matcha for these recipes.

A Word About Allergies

Allergies to wheat, soy, eggs and seafood are very common. Please check with an adult before using an ingredient you are not sure about. READ LABELS CAREFULLY as there may be some ingredients that are new to you.

❶ **Mochiko Rice Flour** This flour is made from grinding sweet rice grains. It is used to make desserts, like everyone's favorite—mochi! It is different from regular rice flour, and there is no substitute for it.

❷ **Sweet Bean Paste** Little red *azuki* beans are boiled with sugar to create a delicious paste (*anko*) that is used in so many Japanese desserts. Although sweetened, it is still bean-based, so it is rich in protein and fiber, and low in fat. It is available in creamy (*koshi-an*) and chunky (*tsubuan*) textures—just like peanut butter!

❸ **Japonica Rice** A short-to-medium-grain variety of rice that when cooked has a sticky, but not mushy texture. It can be picked up easily with chopsticks, rolled into sushi and molded into rice balls or cute sculpted rice characters. It is often called "sushi rice" outside of Japan.

❹ **Nori Furikake** Rice topping sprinkles can be made from a variety of ingredients. It comes in jars or packets and is sprinkled on top of rice to add flavor, color and texture. It is also delicious on pasta and fish. See the recipe on page 43 to make your own!

❺ **Yukari** Dried red *shiso* leaves with salt that has a tangy flavor. Crumble to add beautiful purple sprinkles to rice or pasta.

SEAWEED

Seaweed is the most common sea vegetable used in Japanese cooking. It is a very nutritious vegetable with lots of vitamins and minerals.

Wakame seaweed is sold dried and shredded. It must be rehydrated in water or soup. It is popular in *miso* soup and seaweed salad.

❻ Nori (Laver) Roasted seaweed that is most famously used to wrap around plain rice for *onigiri* and sushi rolls, and for making *furikake*.

⓭ Kombu (Kelp) A thick, flat, dried seaweed that comes in wide strips. It is soaked in water to make *kombu* stock, which is used for soups. *Kombu* stock is a good alternative to chicken and beef stocks for vegetarians.

NOODLES

❼ Dried Ramen Thin wheat noodles that can be wavy or curly and come in round or square "nests." Some are straight and come in long packages like pasta.

❽ Fresh Ramen Packaged fresh ramen must be refrigerated.

Both dried and fresh ramen are suitable for the recipes in this book. They must be boiled before adding the tasty ramen soup mix. Follow the package instructions for cooking times. Instant noodles are convenient, but we do not use them in our recipes.

⓮ Udon Thick white noodles made from wheat. When cooked, they are chewy and sometimes a bit slippery! Fresh or frozen packages come in single-serving size. The dry noodles come in long packages. Udon noodles are often used in soups and stir-fries.

❾ Inari (Seasoned Tofu Pockets) *Inari* are thin fried tofu pockets that are simmered in a sauce composed of soy sauce, sugar and other ingredients. These pockets are small and have an opening on top to stuff in seasoned sushi rice or plain rice.

❿ Sake (Rice Wine) *Sake* is a fermented alcoholic product made using rice that is used for drinking and in cooking. When cooking with *sake*, it is heated until all the alcohol has evaporated. We do not call for using *sake* in this cookbook.

⓫ Dark Sesame Oil This oil is made from pressing roasted sesame seeds. It has a toasty smell and adds a rich, nutty flavor to food.

⓬ Tofu Tofu is made from heated soy milk that has a thickener added. It can then be fried and used in soups, salads and stews. Tofu comes in several textures. The basic three are soft, medium and firm. Tofu is a natural substitute for meat because it is rich in protein.

Equipment

You don't need special equipment to cook Japanese food. Electric rice cookers are in just about every Japanese home, as rice is cooked and eaten there every day, but that is not the case outside of Japan. It is convenient to have one, but we'll teach you how to make rice on your stovetop (see page 27). Some of the other items are fun to have, like the nori punch and mini vegetable cutters. They add that "extra touch," but they are not essential.

- **a** Measuring Cups
- **b** Measuring Spoons
- **c** Rice Cooker
- **d** Mixing Bowls
- **e** Vegetable peeler
- **f** Spatula
- **g** Grater
- **h** Non-stick 8–10-inch Skillet with Lid
- **i** One- and 2-quart Saucepans with Lids
- **j** Whisk
- **k** Tongs
- **l** Cooking Chopsticks (*Saibashi*) Long chopsticks that are used when stirring or stir-frying and keep hands away from the heat. They are helpful to have, but not necessary.
- **m** A Variety of Other Chopsticks
- **n** Sushi Rolling Mat For *maki* sushi rolls.

Cooking chopsticks

Adult-size chopsticks

Child-size chopsticks

Practice chopsticks

- **o** Mini Vegetable Cutters
- **p** Silicone Cups
- **q** Nori Punch For seaweed.
- **r** Small Scissors
- **s** Cute (*Kawaii*) Picks
- **t** Cupcake Liners

19

Safety First in the Kitchen!

- Always get permission from an adult before you cook.
- Always work with an adult when using a knife or vegetable peeler.
- Always work with an adult when using the stovetop or oven.
- Cover your hair.
- Use separate cutting boards for vegetables and raw meats, fish and chicken.
- Wash utensils with detergent and hot water after contact with raw meats, fish or chicken.

Good Practices While Cooking

- Always wash your hands before starting.
- Keep your work surface clean.
- Prepare all the ingredients for a recipe in advance so they're ready to use.
- Remove dirty dishes from the work area and stack them in the sink.
- If you taste something with a spoon, do not put that spoon back in the pot. Put it in the sink. If you want to taste again, get a clean spoon.

Count to Ten in Japanese While Cleaning All Parts of Your Hands!

Learn to count to ten in Japanese while thoroughly cleaning your hands! This helps protect you and others from getting sick. Follow the images and count out loud to ten. Each movement is performed on both hands.

ICHI 1, NI 2, SAN 3, SHI 4, GO 5, ROKU 6, SHICHI 7, HACHI 8, KYU 9, JYU 10

Basic Cooking Techniques

How to Measure

DRY MEASURES—CUPS AND SPOONS
Mound up your measuring cup or spoon with a dry ingredient like flour or sugar. Then, hold it over a bowl and skim across the top with a chopstick or the flat side of a table knife, letting the excess fall into a separate bowl. The surface of the ingredient you are measuring will now be flat, and the portion will be precise.

LIQUID MEASURES
Use a glass or plastic measuring pitcher set flat on the counter to measure liquid. Pour the liquid into the pitcher. Check the markings on the side of the pitcher for the right amount.

MEASURING SPOONS
Before pouring liquid to measure by spoonful, put a small bowl under the spoon to catch any spillage and then pour the liquid into the spoon; then you are ready to use it for the recipe!

How to Cut the Ingredients

HOW TO CUT SAFELY

Using knives safely is very important.

❶ When you use a knife to cut, make sure you are working on a flat cutting board.
❷ Curl the fingers of your non-dominant hand into your palm like a "cat's paw."
❸ Place your "paw" on the edge of the ingredient you are cutting, to hold it steady.
❹ Hold your knife in the other hand and, while cutting the food, keep moving your "paw" back, away from the knife.

• Please choose a knife appropriate for the age and skill level of the young person.

Vegetable cutters (which also work on cheese, deli meat and fruit!) are cute, but have sharp edges—so take care! Cut vegetables like cucumbers ("cukes") and carrots into ¼-inch (6-mm) thick discs first, then center your cutter and press down. For young children, carrots can be softened by microwaving them for 30 seconds.

Slice

Dice

Grate

CUTTING TERMS

Slice Cut into thin, similar-size pieces. It is a good idea to first cut the food in half lengthwise and then lay the flat side down on the cutting board surface. It is easier and safer to cut slices in this way.

Cut into Matchsticks Cut food into thin rounds and then stack a few slices and cut into strips ("matchsticks").

Dicing Cut into roughly cubic portions—small, medium or large. Cut long matchstick pieces and then cut across into cubes.

Mince Cut into tiny pieces. Cut matchsticks and then cut them into very small pieces.

Chop Cut into bite-size pieces.

Grate Hold a microplane or cheese grater over a bowl or plate and rub the ingredient back and forth against the holes of the tool. Carefully control how you hold the food and don't let it get too close to your fingers!

Slice   Dice   Grate

23

CHAPTER 1

JAPANESE RICE

日本のお米

Japanese rice is grown in fields flooded with water, called *paddies*. The baby stalks are planted in the spring and harvested in the fall. *Okome* (oh-koh-may), is a short- or medium-grain rice of the *japonica* variety. It is sometimes referred to as "sushi rice." It is used to make sushi because it is sticky. But it only becomes "sushi rice" after a vinegar and sugar dressing is added.

Rice came to Japan from China over a thousand years ago. It is a *staple* in Japan, which means it is eaten in some form every day; sometimes for breakfast, lunch and dinner! So many foods are made from rice: rice vinegar, rice crackers, rice wine, rice noodles and more.

In this chapter, you will learn how to properly prepare short- or medium-grain rice on the stovetop. Rice appears in many recipes in the book: *donburi*—rice bowls with toppings, *maki* sushi rolls, fried rice with veggies… even rice that has been molded and decorated to become cute characters.

Let's Make Japanese Rice (Gohan)

Japanese rice, sometimes called "sushi rice," is a short- or medium-grain variety. Uncooked, it is called *okome*. When cooked, it is *gohan*, and has a sticky quality that enables it to be picked up with chopsticks or molded into *onigiri* (rice balls) or sushi rolls.

The method to prepare and cook the rice is important for good results:
Rinse. Drain.
Rinse. Drain.
Rinse. Drain.
Soak...
Let me explain!

There is starchy powder on the rice that should be rinsed off. After, rinsing several times, the water should be mostly clear—not cloudy. Then, the rinsed rice is left to soak in water, which helps it to cook to just the right texture. If you have time, please don't skip this step.

If you are using a rice cooker, follow the manufacturer's instructions and see our explanation on the opposite page, but still follow the rinse-and-soak method described here.

METHOD

❶ Place the rice in a strainer and set it into a large bowl or pan.

❷ Fill the bowl or pan with water and swish the rice around with your hand. Remove the strainer holding the rice, discard the cloudy water and repeat two more times.

❸ Refill the pot with water. Set the strainer back in and soak the rice for 20 minutes.

❹ Lift the strainer. Discard water. The rice will be white and ready to cook.

26 Chapter 1

Stovetop Rice

Makes about 4½ cups (800 g)   **Prep time:** 5 mins, plus 20 mins to soak   **Cook time:** 30 minutes

INGREDIENTS

- 2 cups (400 g) Japanese rice, short- or medium-grain white rice ("sushi rice")
- 2 cups, plus 2 tablespoons (about 500 ml) water

Using a Rice Cooker

If you have a rice cooker, follow the recipe below for making the rice (but still follow the rinse-and-soak preparation).

METHOD

❶ Prepare the rice according to the instructions on page 26. Add the rice and water to a medium saucepan with a lid that has a vent. Cover the pot with the lid and cook over medium heat for 8 minutes until it comes to a boil.

❷ With the lid still in place, turn the heat to low and cook for 10 more minutes. If your lid is glass, you will notice small openings appearing on the surface of the mixture.

❸ Turn the heat off and let the rice sit covered for 10 more minutes.

❹ The rice is ready to eat or use in a recipe!

❶ Use the measuring cup that came with the appliance. Rinse and soak the rice according to the instructions on page 26.*

❷ Fill the pot with water to the appropriate level indicated inside the cooker.

❸ Turn the cooker on. The rice will cook and the cooker will shut off when it is done.

*"Smart" rice cookers automatically soak the rice. Please refer to your manual.

Japanese Rice

Rice Balls (Onigiri) Three Ways

Onigiri rice balls are the perfect portable snack. Making them with sticky Japanese rice enables you to mold them into shapes. Triangles are traditional, but they can also be shaped into a ball or a log or a *kawaii* (cute) creature! And you can add different fillings, like tuna, pickled plum or even fried shrimp.

1. Tuna Mayo Rice Balls (Onigiri)

Add Tuna Mayo Filling to Rice Balls, shape them, and wrap them with *nori* for easy handling.

Makes 3 rice balls
Prep time: 15 minutes
Cook time: n/a (excludes making the rice)

INGREDIENTS

- 1½ cups (about 250 g) cooked Japanese rice (see pages 26–27), warm
- Dash of salt
- 2 strips nori (roasted seaweed), for wrapping around the rice
- Rice Sprinkles—Nori or Yukari Furikake, store bought or homemade (see page 43) (optional)

Tuna Mayo Filling

This is the most popular filling for *onigiri* in Japan.

INGREDIENTS

- One 5-oz (142-g) can white tuna in water, drained
- 2 tablespoons mayonnaise
- 1 teaspoon soy sauce
- Dash of dark sesame oil and / or hot sauce (optional)

METHOD

❶ Add drained tuna to a bowl.

❷ Add the mayonnaise and soy sauce. Mix to combine. Add the sesame oil and / or hot sauce, if using.

METHOD

NOTE
If you want a plain *onigiri* with no filling, skip steps 2 and 3, and go directly to 4.

❶ Place about ⅓ cup (55 g) warm rice onto plastic wrap draped over a bowl.

❷ Make a dent in the middle of the rice with the back of a spoon and fill it with a tablespoon of the tuna mixture.

❸ Place a tablespoon or more of the additional rice on top of the tuna mixture and lightly press to cover.

❹ Sprinkle on the dash of salt. Bring the ends of the plastic wrap up and twist to close. Lightly press to form a ball.

❺ Gently shape into a triangle.

❻ Open the wrap. Then, center a strip of seaweed, rough side against the rice, and wrap it around to the other side. Dab one side into Rice Sprinkles, if using, to finish. Make 3 *onigiri*.

Japanese Rice 29

2. Kawaii Rice Balls (Onigiri)

In Japan, you often find rice balls in fun shapes in kids' lunchboxes. *Kawaii* means "cute," so these *onigiri* are yummy and cute! Turn *onigiri* into your own creations. Vegetables like corn, peas and carrots are great for making features for your creatures! Try a chick, panda and penguin. You can dip the back of the rice ball animals into rice sprinkles for more flavor. Today, you can find so many options on the internet. These little critters inspired us!

Kawaii Chick Onigiri

Peep! Peep! This precious chick is looking cheerful with a corn-kernel beak and red-pepper comb. Dots of ketchup make rosy cheeks.

Makes 2 rice balls
Prep time: 10 minutes
Cook time: n/a (excludes making the rice)

INGREDIENTS

- 2 Onigiri (cooked and pressed Japanese rice, sprinkled with a dash of salt)
- 4 corn kernels
- 1 small piece nori (roasted seaweed)
- 1 teaspoon ketchup
- Carrot pieces or red pepper strips
- Rice Sprinkles—Nori or Yukari Furikake, store bought or homemade (see page 43) (optional)

How to make Kawaii Chick Onigiri

METHOD

❶ Shape the wrapped rice into a triangle or oval. Cut eyes and feet from nori and set into place.

❷ Make an indentation with the tip of a chopstick. Tuck in two corn kernels.

❸ Cut a piece of red pepper into a heart shape using scissors. Poke a small hole at top of the head and insert the base of the heart.

❹ Dip the tip of a chopstick into ketchup and dot each cheek to complete. Dab the back into Rice Sprinkles, if using. Make 2 Chicks.

Kawaii Panda Onigiri

White rice and dark nori make the perfect panda! Use a small pair of scissors to cut out your panda's features.

Makes 2 rice balls   **Prep time:** 10 minutes   **Cook time:** n/a (excludes making the rice)

INGREDIENTS

- 2 Onigiri (cooked and pressed Japanese rice, sprinkled with a dash of salt)
- 1 small piece nori (roasted seaweed)
- Rice Sprinkles—Nori or Yukari Furikake, store bought or homemade (see page 43) (optional)

How to make Kawaii Panda Onigiri

METHOD

❶ Shape warm rice into an oval using plastic wrap. With scissors, cut out a nose, 2 eyes, 2 ears, 2 paws and a belt.

❷ Remove the plastic wrap. Use a pair of tweezers or the tip of your finger to place the panda's features onto the rice.

❸ Dab the back into Rice Sprinkles, if using. Make 2 Pandas.

Kawaii Penguin Onigiri

You will need a square of *nori* for creating the face of the penguin. Corn makes a cute beak.

Makes 2 rice balls   **Prep time:** 10 minutes   **Cook time:** n/a (excludes making the rice)

INGREDIENTS

- 2 Onigiri (cooked and pressed Japanese rice, sprinkled with a dash of salt)
- ½ sheet nori (roasted seaweed)
- 4 green peas
- 4 corn kernels
- 1 teaspoon ketchup

How to make Kawaii Penguin Onigiri

METHOD

❶ Shape rice into a ball using plastic wrap. Flatten the ball to form the penguin's face.

❷ Fold the *nori* in half. Cut out the shape of half a heart. Remove and save the heart shape. Unfold the *nori* sheet.

❸ Make a small diagonal snip in each of the 4 corners.

❹ With the "face" on the plastic wrap, place the *nori* square, rough side down, onto the rice.

❺ Flip the *onigiri* over so the heart-shaped opening is facing down.

❻ Twist the plastic wrap around the head to adhere the nori to the rice. Unwrap. Place the cut-out heart-shaped *nori* on the back of the penguin's head.

❼ Set the peas in the face. Press a chopstick tip in the middle of the face and then add corn kernels. Dot the cheeks with ketchup. Make 2 Penguins.

3. Crispy Soy Sauce Glazed Rice Balls (Yaki Onigiri)

Plain *onigiri* grilled in a skillet and brushed with soy sauce is a popular and crispy treat! A mix of *miso* and *mirin* is also a tasty glaze.

Makes 2 rice balls **Prep time:** 5 minutes **Cook time:** 5 minutes (excludes making the rice)

INGREDIENTS

- 2 Onigiri (cooked and pressed Japanese rice, sprinkled with a dash of salt)
- 1 teaspoon oil
- 1–2 teaspoons soy sauce

METHOD

❶ Add the oil to a non-stick skillet. Spread it over the surface of the pan with a paper towel.

❷ Set the pan over medium heat and let it get warm for about 30 seconds.

❸ Add the *onigiri* to the pan and heat them for about 1 minute. Turn them over and heat for another minute. Reduce heat to medium low.

❹ Brush soy sauce over the surface of the *onigiri*. Flip the *onigiri* and heat them on low for another minute. Be careful not to burn the rice.

❺ Brush both sides with soy sauce a second time. Continue flipping until they have a toasty brown color. Serve warm.

Japanese Rice   33

Rice Sandwiches (Onigirazu)

Onigirazu is a rice sandwich wrapped with nori! It became popular from the manga (comic book series) *Cooking Papa*. The Papa is a great cook and each story is related to food and even includes recipes. *Onigirazu* became a fad in Japan! Try different types of food combinations. Don't overstuff and don't worry if it is a little sloppy. Once you wrap and cut, it all works out!

Makes 2   **Prep time:** 10 minutes   **Cook time:** 5 minutes (for the eggs—excludes making the rice)

Ham, Egg, Cheese and Cucumber Filling

INGREDIENTS

- 2 eggs
- 2 teaspoons oil
- 1 green onion (scallion), sliced into small rings (green part) (optional)
- 2 sheets nori (roasted seaweed)
- 1½ cups (250 g) cooked Japanese rice (see pages 26–27)
- 2 slices Havarti, Muenster, cheddar or American cheese
- 2 slices baked ham, cut in half
- 1 mini or Persian cucumber, sliced thinly on a diagonal
- 2 tablespoons mayonnaise

34 Chapter 1

How to make the sandwiches

METHOD

❶ Beat the eggs in a bowl. Add the oil to a small skillet over medium heat. Add the eggs and distribute them by rotating the pan. Sprinkle with chopped green onions, if using. Cook until just set. Turn out onto a plate to cool.

❷ Once the eggs are cool, fold the omelet and cut in half. Arrange the fillings on a plate.

❸ Tear off a 10-in (25-cm) piece of plastic wrap and place it on cutting board. Put a sheet of *nori* down, rough side up. Place about ⅓ cup (55 g) of rice in the center of the seaweed and spread it into a 3-in (7.5-cm) square. Spread with ½ tablespoon of mayonnaise.

❹ Layer 1 slice of cheese, ½ slice of ham, half of the omelet and top with about half of the cucumbers.

❺ Spread with ½ tablespoon of mayonnaise and top with about ⅓ cup (55 g) of rice. Gently spread the rice to cover. Lift a corner of the *nori* and begin wrapping the contents like an envelope! Bring one corner of the seaweed over the fillings and hold with your finger. Continue around, folding and overlapping until covered. Wrap tightly in plastic wrap. Set aside for 5 minutes.

❻ Wet a paper towel and set it on the counter. Swipe the front and back of a knife blade over the towel to moisten it. Slice the sandwich in half. Remove the plastic wrap and enjoy!

Chicken and Egg Rice Bowls (Oyako Donburi)

Which came first? The chicken or the egg? We don't know either, but they come together in this rice bowl meal! Chunks of chicken simmer and become tasty and tender in a sauce composed of typical Japanese seasonings: soy sauce, sugar and *mirin*. Here, we call for chicken thighs to be used, as the dark meat is more flavorful than white breast meat. Beaten eggs form a velvety topping. Once set, spoon the rich broth over rice, and you have a meal!

Serves 2–4 **Prep time:** 20 minutes **Cook time:** 15 minutes (excludes making the rice)

INGREDIENTS

- 1 medium onion
- 2–3 eggs, beaten (if you like your bowl to be eggy, use 3 eggs)
- 1 cup (250 ml) water or chicken stock
- 2 tablespoons soy sauce
- 1½ tablespoons sugar
- 2 tablespoons mirin
- ½ lb (225 g) chicken thighs, cut into 1-in (2.5-cm) pieces
- 1 green onion (scallion), trimmed, green and white parts, cut into 6 pieces
- 2 cups (325 g) cooked Japanese rice (see pages 26–27)

NOTE
Use separate cutting boards for meat and veggies. When you are done cutting the chicken, it is important to wash your hands and the cutting board with hot water and soap.

36 Chapter 1

How to make the Chicken and Egg Rice Bowl

METHOD

❶ Trim the ends of the onion, peel it, and cut it in half from top to bottom. Lay half an onion on a cutting board with the flat side down. Cut thin slices crosswise, into a half-moon shapes.

❷ Place the beaten eggs next to the stove.

❸ Add the water or chicken stock to an 8-in (20-cm) skillet. Add the soy sauce, sugar and *mirin* and mix well. Heat over medium heat until bubbles begin to appear.

❹ Add the onions to the soy sauce mixture and cook for 1 minute until the onions begin to soften.

❺ Add the chicken and green onion pieces and cook for 4–5 minutes, or until the chicken is done.

❻ Stir the eggs and slowly pour them, little by little, in a circle over the chicken. Cook for 1 minute, turn off the heat and let sit for another minute. The eggs will be soft but set.

❼ Divide the rice into 2 bowls. With a ladle, scoop up the chicken mixture and pour it over the rice in equal portions. Serve warm.

Japanese Rice 37

CHAPTER 2

FLAVORS FROM THE SEA

海の恵み

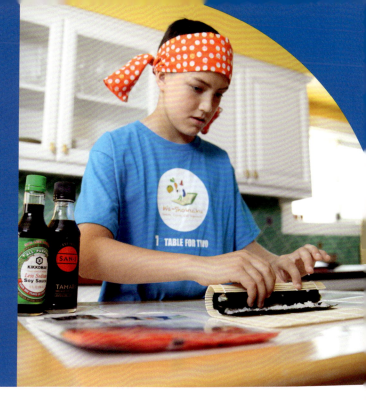

Japan is an island nation, which means it is surrounded by the ocean. So naturally, the ocean is one of their major sources for food. Fish for protein and sea vegetables for minerals are both mainstays of the Japanese diet.

Snacks made with *nori* (crispy sheets of dried seaweed) are very popular outside Japan. In Japan, *nori* is mostly used to wrap around rice or used to make *onigiri*, or sushi rolls like our Tuna and Cucumber Sushi Rolls (page 50). *Nori* is also used to make tasty rice sprinkles that add flavor to rice or pump up popcorn, like we demonstrate on page 44. There are many seaweed varieties, such as *wakame*, used in salads or added to *miso* soups, and *kombu* (kelp), for making the very important soup stock called *dashi*.

Seaweed is full of vitamin E, which keeps your hair shiny, as well as minerals like magnesium and calcium, that help your bones stay healthy and grow. Fish like salmon, tuna and mackerel are good sources of low-fat protein that builds muscles and encourages brain development.

Try the Teriyaki Salmon Bowls (page 48) with chunks of vegetables topped with a delicious sauce, or delight your family with a bowl of refreshing chilled Japanese-style Tuna Pasta (page 53) tossed in a tangy sauce.

Make Your Own Chopstick Rests (箸置き)

Chopstick rests (*hashioki*) are an important part of Japanese table settings. Place chopsticks horizontally in front of the plate with the tips resting on the *hashioki* to your left. This keeps the tips clean and makes the chopsticks easy to pick up—if you are a "righty!" There are many cool chopstick rest shapes and designs.

SUGGESTED MATERIALS
- Decorative, heavy (glossy) paper from a gift bag, wrapping paper or colored origami paper
- Transparent tape, or *Washi* tape (decorative masking tape)
- Scissors

The Roll
❶ Cut a strip approximately 8-in (20-cm) long and 1-in (2.5-cm) wide from paper of your choice.

❷ Roll the paper away from you into log. Tape the end closed.

40 Chapter 2

The Japanese Knot

This works best if the paper is lighter in weight (such as origami paper) and the same pattern is printed on both sides.

❶ We used 6¾-in (17-cm) origami paper. Fold the paper in half, edge to edge. Unfold, and then cut along the crease.

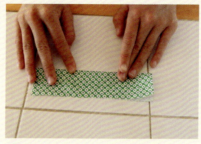

❷ Using one of the rectangles from step ❶, fold the paper in half, long edge to long edge.

❸ Fold the paper into thirds. Then, bend the paper near the middle.

❹ Cross the left strip over the right side, leaving an open loop in the middle. Bring the left strip under the right strip and up through the middle of the space.

❺ Gently pull the paper straight up. You will have a sharp corner at the top. The ends do not have to be even. It is even better if they are knot. (Ha, ha!)

❻ Turn the knot over and tuck each end under the main strip (or trim the ends with scissors, if you prefer).

LOOK
How many chopstick rests you can find throughout the book? Search for animals and *kawaii* things!

You have made a Japanese knot chopstick rest!

Flavors from the Sea

Dashi Soup Stock

There are two commonly used soup stocks in Japanese cooking. Both are based on food from the sea. One is made with dried bonito fish flakes (*katsuobushi*) and kelp (*kombu*) and the other with just kelp—which is vegetarian. Sometimes dried *shiitake* mushrooms and *daikon* radish are added to the seaweed.

   Dashi is the base for many sauces and soups, like *miso* soup, and is easy and quick to make from scratch. There are also instant powder packets available for both. If you are unable to obtain the ingredients, substitute vegetable or chicken stock.

Makes about 1 quart (1 liter)

Kombu Dashi

This stock is mild and tastes like the ocean. It is healthy and vegan. There are two ways to make this clear stock.

METHOD

REFRIGERATOR METHOD

Fill a large jar with 4 cups (1 liter) of water. Put a 3-in (7.5-cm) piece of kombu in the jar. Close the lid and place the jar in the refrigerator for at least 12 hours.

STOVETOP METHOD

❶ Place a 3-in (7.5-cm) piece of kombu in a medium saucepan with 4 cups (1 liter) of water. Let it soak for 20 minutes.

❷ Turn the heat to medium and heat the seaweed until it just begins to simmer. With a pair of tongs, remove the seaweed and discard it.

Bonito Dashi

METHOD

❶ Place 4 cups (1 liter) of water in a medium saucepan. Add a 3-in (7.5-cm) piece of kombu and let it soak for 20 minutes.

❷ Turn the heat to medium and heat the water until it just begins to simmer. With a pair of tongs, remove the seaweed and discard it.

❸ Take a handful of bonito flakes (about 1 cup) and add it all at once to the simmering water. Turn off the heat. The bonito flakes will sink to the bottom of the pot. Let the flakes steep for about 2 minutes.

❹ Place a mesh strainer over a bowl, pour the stock and bonito flakes into the strainer. Discard the solids. Your *dashi* is ready to use.

Simple Nori Furikake – Tasty Seaweed Rice Sprinkles

Rice sprinkles are bits of *nori* (roasted seaweed) combined with seasonings to create flavorful toppings for rice. There are many blends, but the most popular one consists of *nori*, sesame seeds, sugar and salt. In this homemade recipe, we call for fresh, crisp *nori*, but it is also a good way to use up old *nori* (see tip). *Furikake* is also great sprinkled on pasta and popcorn.

Makes about ½ cup (about 110 g)
Prep time: 10 minutes

TIP
How to Crisp Up Stale Nori
If your *nori* has become chewy through exposure to air, crisp it up by placing it into a medium-size dry skillet over low heat for about 1–2 minutes. If the *nori* is already torn into shreds, constantly stir the pieces with a wooden spoon. This will toast the seaweed, making it crispy again.

INGREDIENTS
- 2–3 sheets nori (roasted seaweed)
- 1 tablespoon toasted sesame seeds
- 2 teaspoons salt
- 2 teaspoons sugar

METHOD

❶ Over a large bowl, tear and crumble seaweed into very small pieces.

❷ Add the sesame seeds and stir to combine.

❸ Add the salt and sugar to the seaweed mixture and mix well. Store in a small glass jar to keep the *nori* crispy for about 2 weeks. The sugar and salt will tend to settle, so shake well before each use.

Flavors from the Sea

Furikake Popcorn

Who doesn't love freshly popped popcorn? Give it a twist by sprinkling on your favorite Japanese rice sprinkles. Drizzle a small amount of melted butter or oil (or use a sprayable oil) over top to help the *furikake* seasoning stay put.

Makes approximately 6 cups
Prep time: 5 minutes
Cook time: 10 minutes

INGREDIENTS

- 1½ tablespoons oil
- ¼ cup (about 35 g) popping corn kernels
- 2 tablespoons butter
- 2–3 tablespoons Simple Nori Furikake (see page 43), or store-bought furikake, divided

METHOD

STOVETOP METHOD

❶ Pour the oil into a deep saucepan or skillet that has a lid. Add 1 kernel of corn. Heat over medium heat.

❷ When the kernel pops, add the remaining kernels. Cover with the lid and gently shake the pan back and forth until the remaining kernels have mostly stopped popping.

❸ Remove from the heat and wait about 30 seconds before you take off the cover.

❹ Place the butter in a 1-cup (250-ml) glass measuring cup and microwave for 45 seconds. Add time by 15 seconds, if necessary, until the butter has melted completely. Or, melt the butter in a small pan over low heat on the stovetop.

❺ Drizzle the butter over the popcorn. Toss with a big spoon while sprinkling on 1 tablespoon of the *furikake*, mixing it into the popcorn. Sprinkle the remaining tablespoon of the *furikake* on top.

HOT AIR POPCORN POPPER METHOD

❶ Make your popcorn following the popper instructions, and then follow the directions from step ❹ above.

If you are using pre-popped corn from a bag, you can still season with *furikake* by adding some melted butter or spray oil before adding the sprinkles.

Nori Jam (Tsukudani)

If you find yourself with stale *nori* seaweed on your hands, don't discard it (*mottainai*, "what a waste")—prepare this delicious condiment instead! It's used as a topping for hot plain white rice or as *onigiri* filling. Spread it on toast for a savory treat or mix it with hot pasta. Can you think of other tasty combinations to try? Keep a jar of this jam in the fridge so it's ready whenever inspiration strikes.

Makes about ½ cup (125 g)
Prep time: 20 mins (incl. rest)
Cook time: 5–8 minutes (excludes making the rice)

INGREDIENTS

- 5–6 sheets of nori (roasted seaweed)
- 3 tablespoons soy sauce
- 2 tablespoons mirin
- 1 tablespoon sugar
- ½ cup (125 ml) water—as needed

METHOD

❶ Rip or cut up 5–6 sheets of roasted seaweed into small pieces and place them into a small saucepan.

❷ Add the soy sauce, *mirin* and sugar. Stir to combine. Let the mixture rest for about 15 minutes.

❸ Move the pan to the stove and heat it over medium-low heat, stirring the mixture until the *nori* has absorbed all the seasonings and begins to soften.

❹ Add half of the water and simmer over low heat for about 3 minutes. Stir frequently. Continue to add water, little by little, to keep the mixture the consistency of a jam. Allow the jam to cool, and then transfer it to a small glass jar. Store in the refrigerator for up to 1 month.

Flavors from the Sea

Salmon and Vegetables in Miso Sauce
(Chan Chan Yaki)

This dish is from the northern island of Hokkaido, where salmon is a specialty. "Chan chan" represents the sound of a spatula hitting an iron grill, which is what this dish was said to be cooked on in Japan. We use foil pouches to wrap the salmon and vegetables together and cook them in a simmering water bath. When the fish and vegetables are done, the pouches serve as plates! Serve with rice, and spoon the delicious sauce over top.

Serves 2 **Prep time:** 20 minutes **Cook time:** 15–20 minutes

INGREDIENTS

- ½ lb (250 g) skinless salmon filet or ½ block (about 165 g) firm tofu, drained
- Salt, for sprinkling
- 4 cabbage leaves
- 6 fresh shiitake mushrooms (or brown or white mushrooms)
- ½ bunch shimeji (beech) mushrooms (or mushroom of your choice)
- ½ medium onion, thinly sliced
- ½ cup (65 g) canned, frozen or fresh corn kernels
- 2 tablespoons butter
- 1½–2 cups cooked Japanese rice (see pages 26–27), hot

MISO SAUCE
- 3 tablespoons shiro (white) miso paste (mild)
- 2 tablespoons mirin or 1 tablespoon sugar
- 2 tablespoons water
- 1 teaspoon soy sauce

METHOD

1. Cut the salmon in half lengthwise into 2 equal pieces. Sprinkle with salt. Set aside. If using tofu, cut the block in half and wrap it in paper towels for 10 minutes. Lightly fry the tofu pieces in a skillet with a small amount of oil. Set aside.

2. Remove the ribs from the cabbage leaves and cut the leaves into 2-in (5-cm) pieces. Slice the *shiitake* mushrooms into ½-in (1.25-cm) pieces. Pull apart the cluster of shimeji mushrooms.

3. Lay 2 pieces of foil (10 in / 25 cm) side by side. Add parchment paper (10 in / 25 cm) on top. Divide the cabbage pieces in half and lay a bed of cabbage on each piece of paper. Pile on the sliced mushrooms, onions and the corn. Top each vegetable mound with the salmon or fried tofu.

4. Make the Miso Sauce: in a bowl, add the *miso*, *mirin*, water and soy sauce. Stir the ingredients to combine them. Spoon half of the *miso* sauce on top of each piece of salmon (or tofu) and vegetables.

5. Cut the butter into several pieces and dot them on top of the salmon (or tofu) pieces.

6. Make the foil packages: bring the two edges of foil to meet and fold them over together. Crimp the ends. Don't make the package too tight.

7 Add about 2 in (5 cm) of warm water to the bottom of a medium-skillet with a lid. Place over medium heat. When the water begins to simmer, place the foil packages in the water. The water should come almost halfway up the height of the packets. Put the lid on the skillet and cook for about 10 minutes. Add more water to the pan as needed to replace water that has evaporated. Cook for another 5–10 minutes.

8 Carefully remove the packets from the skillet, placing one on each plate. Very carefully open the packets to release the steam. Serve hot with the rice.

Flavors from the Sea 47

Teriyaki Salmon Bowls

Rice bowls with a variety of toppings are called *donburi* in Japanese and are easy to prepare. Our friends, Hugo, 11 and Bruno, 7, prepared this meal in a bowl for their parents. "This is the most fun I've ever had cooking, and it's really delicious!" exclaimed Bruno. Hugo agreed as he went for seconds! We make this rice bowl with salmon, but it would be delicious with chicken too.

Zucchini is not a traditional ingredient in Japanese cooking, but it adds color and veggie goodness to the meal! Use one skillet to cook both the salmon and zucchini for easy-peasy cleanup.

Serves 4 **Prep time:** 15 mins, plus 10 mins to salt **Cook time:** 10 minutes (excludes making the rice)

INGREDIENTS

- 1 lb (500 g) skinless salmon filet, cut into 2-in (5-cm) cubes
- Salt, for sprinkling
- ½ tablespoon oil
- 1 tablespoon butter, divided
- 1 medium zucchini (about 150 g), green or yellow, cut into 1-in (2.5-cm) cubes
- 5 tablespoons Teriyaki Sauce (see page 60), plus more for topping
- 3–4 cups cooked Japanese rice (see pages 26–27)

METHOD

1. Sprinkle the salmon cubes with a little salt and set aside for 10 minutes.

2. Add the oil and ½ tablespoon of the butter to a non-stick skillet and, over medium heat, heat the butter and oil until sizzling. Add the zucchini and cook for 3 minutes. With a slotted spoon, transfer the zucchini cubes from the pan and set aside.

3. Add the remaining butter and let it melt. Add the salmon cubes and cook for 2 minutes. With a pair of tongs, turn the fish over and cook for 1 more minute. With a slotted spoon, transfer the salmon from the pan and set it aside.

4. Turn off the heat and wipe the skillet clean with a paper towel. Add the Teriyaki Sauce to the skillet and return it to medium heat. Bring it to a boil for 30 seconds. Reduce the heat to low.

5. Using tongs, add the salmon to the simmering Teriyaki sauce and cook for 1 minute, gently turning the fish to evenly coat the cubes. With a slotted spoon, remove the salmon and set aside.

6. Divide the rice among the bowls. Add the zucchini and salmon. Drizzle on a tablespoon of Teriyaki sauce to top each bowl. Serve hot.

Flavors from the Sea   49

Tuna and Cucumber Sushi Rolls (Maki)

Sushi rolls are easier to make than you think. You can use plain cooked short- or medium-grain rice, or you can make sushi rice with a dressing of rice vinegar, sugar and salt. When added to warm rice, this dressing adds flavor, but it also acts as a preservative and helps to keep the food safe to eat.

Successful sushi-roll making requires that you prepare all your ingredients in advance and lay them out on the work surface in front of you. Disposable plastic gloves are useful for keeping your hands clean while spreading the rice.

Makes 3 rolls—24 pieces   **Prep time:** 25 minutes   **Cook time:** n/a (excludes making the rice)

INGREDIENTS

- 3 sheets nori (roasted seaweed)
- 2 cups (325 g) cooked Japanese rice (see pages 26–27)
- Tuna Mayo Filling recipe, doubled (see page 28)
- 2 mini cucumbers cut into strips, skin-on or English cucumber
- Soy sauce, for dipping

TIP
Prepare a small dish of water. Wet the tip of your finger and dab it on the *nori* at the top where there is no rice.

50   Chapter 2

How to make and cut maki

METHOD

❶ Lay roasted seaweed shiny-side down on a sushi rolling mat. Spread ½ cup of the rice.

❷ Deposit a line of Tuna Mayo Filling across the center of the rice.

❸ Lay the cucumbers alongside the tuna.

❹ Lift the mat over the tuna and cukes and apply light pressure.

❺ Lift the mat and continue to roll forward slowly. Careful! Don't roll the mat inside. When the roll is complete, wrap the mat around the log and lightly apply pressure.

❻ Unwrap. You made a *maki* sushi roll!

❼ Wet a paper towel and lay it on the counter. Moisten the blade of the knife by swiping it against the paper towel before each cut. Cut the roll into 8 pieces, starting in the middle, and then dividing each half into halves, then halve again. Serve with a small portion of soy sauce on the side.

Flavors from the Sea 51

Wakame, Cucumber and Cherry Tomato Salad

Wakame is a type of seaweed that is often served in soups and salads. It is sold dried in packages. To make salad you have to rehydrate it, which means adding water to the seaweed to soften it—no cooking necessary. A small amount goes a long way! Just two tablespoons of the dried seaweed are enough for four people! These salads are served in small bowls as part of a meal. Seaweed is a healthy addition with lots of vitamins and minerals, particularly vitamin E.

Serves 4
Prep time: 10 minutes

INGREDIENTS

- 2 tablespoons dried wakame
- 1 cup (250 ml) water
- 6 cherry tomatoes, cut into quarters
- 1 mini cucumber, thinly sliced
- ½ teaspoon salt, divided
- 1 tablespoon rice vinegar
- 2 teaspoons sugar
- Soy sauce, to taste

METHOD

❶ Place the *wakame* in a bowl and cover it with the water. After about 5 minutes, pour the expanded *wakame* into a strainer.

❷ Roughly chop the rehydrated *wakame* and put it into a mixing bowl.

❸ Add the quartered cherry tomatoes to the *wakame*.

❹ Place the sliced cucumbers in a bowl and sprinkle on ¼ teaspoon of the salt. Let it sit for 5 minutes. Gather the cucumbers in your hand and squeeze out the liquid. Add them to the cherry tomatoes and *wakame*.

❺ Mix the rice vinegar, sugar and the remaining ¼ teaspoon of the salt in a small bowl until the sugar and salt are dissolved. Spoon half of the dressing over the salad. Add a dash or two of soy sauce. Mix and taste. Add more dressing if necessary.

Japanese-style Tuna Pasta

Tuna and pasta tossed with Japanese-style dressing makes a delicious dish served at room temperature. Add *nori* (roasted seaweed) cut into slivers for more taste of the sea. The dressing recipe makes more than you need for this dish, so save the unused portion to drizzle over fresh sliced cucumbers for a quick, refreshing salad.

Serves 4
Prep time: 10 minutes
Cook time: 12 minutes (for the pasta)

INGREDIENTS

- ½ lb (225 g) uncooked spaghetti
- ¼ cup (65 ml) oil
- 3 tablespoons rice vinegar
- 3 tablespoons soy sauce
- 2 teaspoons sugar
- 1 tablespoon mirin
- Pinch of salt
- One 5-oz (142-g) can tuna (in water), drained
- 1 green onion (scallion), trimmed and sliced diagonally
- 10 cherry tomatoes, cut in half
- ½ sheet nori (roasted seaweed)
- Toasted sesame seeds, for sprinkling

METHOD

1. Prepare the pasta according to the package directions. Drain and place in a serving bowl or on a platter. Set aside.

2. Whisk together the oil, rice vinegar, soy sauce, sugar, *mirin* and salt in a bowl.

3. Pour half of the dressing over the pasta and toss until thoroughly mixed.

4. Spread the tuna and green onions evenly over the top of the pasta. Add the cherry tomatoes. Drizzle about 2 tablespoons of the remaining dressing over the top.

5. Fold the nori into a 2-in (5-cm) square. Holding the nori over the pasta, cut thin strips over the top of the pasta with a pair of scissors.

6. Sprinkle on the toasted sesame seeds and serve.

Flavors from the Sea

CHAPTER 3

FOOD FROM SOY

大豆

The humble, but mighty soybean is an important part of Japanese food culture. Soybeans are packed with protein, which helps you grow. Sometimes referred to as the "meat of the fields," soybeans are popular with vegetarians everywhere. Like rice, some form of the soybean is used in just about every Japanese meal.

Soy sauce and *tamari*, its gluten-free cousin, are fermented soy-based liquids used for cooking and dressing Japanese food. Savory *miso* paste is used for making soups and dips. In solid form, there are blocks of tofu.

Tofu is a "blank canvas," meaning you can add all sorts of different seasonings to it and get great results. Add little tofu cubes to the Miso Soup with Vegetables (page 61) for a double hit of soy. Or, make delicious Tofu Croquettes (page 62) using ginger, soy sauce and panko breadcrumbs.

Baby soybeans, known as *edamame*, have become a favorite healthy snack outside of Japan, and can be found in the frozen food section in your local supermarket. Pop them into your mouth, or use them to top a tofu pocket (page 58). Or, try our simple Crunchy Edamame Rolls (page 57), where edamame and cheese are rolled in a gyoza wrapper and quick-fried to crispy perfection.

Chopsticks Challenge!

Let's try a Chopstick Challenge competition with *edamame*! This is a fun way to practice and gain chopsticks skills. When you are finished, you can even eat the delicious *edamame*. You will need one set of chopsticks and about 20–40 *edamame* per player.

Here are two different challenges you can try for this activity.

Simple Shape Challenge

① Set a timer for 1 minute.

② Move 5 *edamame* with chopsticks to create a circle. Continue making circles of 5 *edamame* for 1 minute, and then count how many you've made.

Creative Competition

① Set a timer for 2 minutes.

② Move *edamame* with chopsticks to make a creative shape.

GUESS
How many foods made with soybeans can you name?

(See page 62 for a list of foods.)

56 Chapter 3

Crunchy Edamame Rolls

You can use gyoza, wonton or spring-roll skins to wrap *edamame* for a crunchy, protein-filled snack. In a pinch, you could even flatten a slice of bread with a rolling pin and use that as the wrapper. These can be baked or fried.

Makes 12 rolls   **Prep time:** 15 minutes   **Cook time:** 3–5 minutes

TIP Edamame is a popular and healthy snack. Find the shelled or in-the-pod beans in the frozen food section at the store. Edamame in the pod is fun to eat. Hold the pod near your mouth with both hands. Squeeze it, and the beans will pop into your mouth!

INGREDIENTS
- 12 wonton, spring roll or gyoza wrappers
- 2 slices cheddar cheese
- 24–36 shelled and boiled edamame
- 1 tablespoon canola oil

METHOD

❶ Have a small dish of water on hand. Place a wrapper on a cutting board or plate. If using a square wonton wrapper, turn it so that it is in a diamond shape in front of you.

❷ Cut each slice of the cheese into 3 strips, and then cut the strips in half to make 12 pieces. Lay one piece of cheese horizontally across the lower third of the wrapper.

❸ Place 2–3 edamame in a line on top of the cheese. Dip a fingertip into the dish of water and then wet the edges of the skin.

❹ From the bottom, fold the tip of the wrapper over the edamame. Fold the right side of the wrapper to the middle, and then fold the left side to the middle, like an open envelope.

❺ Roll the packet away from you until you have formed a log-shaped roll. Make sure the edges are sealed.

TO FRY In a skillet over medium-low heat, heat the oil for about 30 seconds. Add the rolls and fry for about 1 minute on each side until skin is crispy. Drain on a paper towel.

TO BAKE Preheat the oven to 350°F (175°C). Grease a shallow baking dish or cookie sheet. Place the rolls on the dish or sheet. Bake for about 3 minutes on each side until the skin is golden-brown and crispy.

Food from Soy

Rice-stuffed Tofu Pockets (Inari Sushi)

Here is a popular type of sushi for picnics, *bento* boxes and parties. It is named for shrines where foxes were said to feed on the tofu pouches left as offerings. The brown tofu skin makes for a cute teddy bear!

Makes 12 pockets **Prep time:** 30 minutes **Cook time:** n/a (excludes making the rice)

INGREDIENTS

SUSHI RICE DRESSING
- 3 tablespoons rice vinegar
- 1 tablespoon sugar
- ¼ teaspoon salt

- 3 cups (500 g) cooked Japanese rice (see pages 26–27)
- 1 cup (165 g) frozen mixed vegetables (carrots, peas and corn), thawed
- 12 Inari tofu skins (available at Asian or Japanese grocery stores, or online)

METHOD

If you want to use plain rice, skip steps ❶ and ❷.

❶ Mix the vinegar, sugar and salt in a small bowl. Stir until dissolved.

❷ Place the hot rice in a large bowl. Drizzle on half of the dressing and it fold into the rice. Taste the rice. Add more of the dressing as needed. Do NOT add all of the dressing at once. You may have some dressing left over.

❸ Fold the vegetables into the rice until evenly distributed.

❹ Hold the *inari* pocket in your hand, cut part facing up. With your fingers, carefully spread it open until you have a pocket.

❺ With a small spoon, fill each pocket with 1–2 tablespoons of the rice.

❻ They are ready to eat! If you want to make *kawaii* (cute) bear *inari* sushi, refer to the photo and cut out features from cheese and roasted seaweed!

58 Chapter 3

Miso Dip with Vegetables

Miso makes a great base for a dip. Mix with mayonnaise and yogurt for a creamy texture, and add some simple seasonings to your liking. We think this sweet and salty spread pairs perfectly with a rainbow of crunchy veggies.

Makes about ¾ cup (185 ml) of dip   **Prep time:** 15 minutes

INGREDIENTS

- ¼ cup (125 g) white miso paste (any type will work)
- 2 tablespoons mayonnaise
- 1 tablespoon Greek yogurt
- 1 tablespoon honey
- 1 teaspoon sesame oil (optional)

VEGETABLES

Choose any fresh vegetables that you like. Here are some suggestions:
- ¼ head green cabbage, cored and chopped into 2-in (5-cm) squares
- 2–3 mini cucumbers, washed and cut into ½-in (1.25-cm) slices
- 1 red, yellow or orange bell pepper, washed, seeded and cut into strips
- 1 carrot, cut into strips

METHOD

❶ In a bowl, combine the *miso* paste, mayo, yogurt, honey and sesame oil, if using. Whisk together until well combined.

❷ Arrange vegetables around the *miso* dip and serve.

TIP
Cut vegetables in a variety of shapes and sizes for an interesting looking arrangement. We used a wavy cutter for the carrots. The grooves are great for scooping up more dip!

Food from Soy

Teriyaki Sauce

In Japanese, *teri* means "glaze" and *yaki* means "to grill." Teriyaki sauce, which is brushed onto grilled meats and fish, is one of the most popular Japanese sauces. It is a combination of sweet and salty ingredients that is heated and condensed into a thick glaze. *Mirin*, a mildly sweet rice wine, gives the sauce its shine. The sauce can be used in many different recipes, including the Teriyaki Salmon Bowls (page 48) and the Teriyaki Chicken Meatballs portion of the Okosama Lunch (page 96). Use caution—this mixture will become extremely hot and sticky during preparation. Keep a jar of this in the refrigerator.

Makes ½ cup (125 ml)   **Prep time:** 5 minutes   **Cook time:** about 10 minutes

INGREDIENTS

- 6 tablespoons soy sauce
- 1 tablespoon mirin
- 3 tablespoons white or brown sugar
- 1 tablespoon water

METHOD

❶ Combine the soy sauce, *mirin*, sugar and water in a small saucepan. Stir the mixture over medium heat until it begins to boil.

❷ Reduce the heat to medium low and simmer for about 5 minutes until the sauce begins to thicken. Turn off the heat and let the sauce cool. It is ready to use!

Miso Soup with Vegetables

Tofu, green onions and *wakame* (seaweed) are common ingredients in this popular Japanese soup, but you can add any vegetables you like. We call for using mild "white" (*shiro*) *miso* paste, as it is the least salty. The vegetarian *dashi* stock is made with *kombu* (kelp) seaweed.

Serves 4 **Prep time:** 10 minutes
Cook time: 15 minutes

INGREDIENTS

- One 3-in (7.5-cm) strip of dried kombu (kelp), or 1 packet of kombu dashi powder
- 3 cups water
- 1 carrot, cut into ¼-in (6-mm) thick rounds, half-moons or cut into shapes with a veggie cutter
- 3–4 tablespoons shiro miso paste (or any miso paste)
- ½ block (about ½ lb / 225 g) soft or medium tofu cut into ½-in (1.25-cm) cubes
- 1 tablespoon dried wakame seaweed
- 1 green onion (scallion), trimmed and sliced into thin rings, for garnish

METHOD

❶ Place the *kombu* strip into a saucepan and add the water. Let it soak for 30 minutes. Then, move the pan to the stove and heat it over medium heat. Just before the water boils, remove the *kombu* strip with a fork and reduce the heat to low. (Alternatively, use a packet of powdered *kombu* stock or other commercially prepared stock including *dashi*, vegetable, beef or chicken.)

❷ Add the carrots and simmer for 2 minutes.

❸ Place half of the *miso* paste into a ladle and lower the ladle into the *dashi*. With a spoon or chopstick, and with your hand positioned high above the hot soup, mix the paste into the soup until it melts. Repeat with remaining *miso* paste.

❹ Add the tofu and *wakame* and let them simmer for 1 minute. (Don't boil *miso* soup, as doing so makes it lose flavor!)

❺ Turn off the heat. Divide the soup into bowls and garnish it with the green onions.

Tofu Croquettes

When tofu is thawed after freezing, its consistency completely changes. It looks like a sponge! Press out the liquid and slice for stir fries, or crumble and use instead of ground meat for a vegetarian substitute. Yoko Ho, a Wa-Sho instructor, showed us how to make these crunchy little *croquettes* (fried patties), which are perfect for a snack, dinner, picnic or *bento* box. These can be made with fresh tofu, but you must drain as much water as you can before using (page 105).

Makes 8 pieces   **Prep time:** 15 minutes, plus 15–30 to chill   **Cook time:** 10 minutes

INGREDIENTS

- ½ block (6 oz / 175 g) firm tofu
- ½ teaspoon garlic powder
- One 1-in (2.5-cm) piece fresh ginger, peeled and grated (optional)
- ½ teaspoon soy sauce
- 1 tablespoon all-purpose flour
- 1 egg, beaten
- ½ cup (35 g) Japanese panko, or other breadcrumbs
- 2 tablespoons canola oil
- Ketchup or Easy Homemade Okonomiyaki Sauce (see page 89), for dipping

METHOD

1. Wrap a half block of tofu in plastic wrap or put it in a container with a lid. Place the tofu in the freezer overnight. Remove the tofu from the freezer and set it on the table to defrost for several hours. Once defrosted, over a bowl, lightly press the water from the tofu.

2. Put the tofu in a bowl and gently mash it with a fork. Add the garlic powder, ginger (if using) and soy sauce. Mix well. Sprinkle in the flour and mix until combined.

3. Add the beaten egg to the tofu mash. Mix until the egg is incorporated.

4. Place the panko in a shallow bowl. With a spoon, scoop up about a tablespoon of tofu mash and form a small patty using your hands. Roll it in the panko to coat. Place the patty on a plate. Repeat with remaining tofu mash. Place the coated patties in the refrigerator for about 15–30 minutes to chill.

5. Add the oil to a medium skillet over medium heat. Let the oil heat for about 30 seconds.

6. With a metal spatula, carefully place the croquettes in the hot oil. Cook for about 1 minute on each side until the panko has become light brown.

7. Set a wire cooling rack over a paper towel. Place the patties on the rack briefly to drain. Serve hot with ketchup or Easy Homemade Okonomiyaki Sauce.

PAGE 56 ANSWER KEY:
- soybean oil • soy milk
- miso • tempeh • natto
- soy sauce • tamari
- tofu

Food from Soy 63

CHAPTER 4

VEGETABLES & FRUIT

野菜と果物

Vegetables provide loads of nutrients for our bodies, particularly when eaten in season, at peak ripeness! They come in every color, size and shape, and can be eaten raw or cooked. Veggies provide fiber to keep our bodies functioning, and key vitamins to maintain our health. They play a big part in Japanese cuisine.

Traditional Japanese meals often contain one soup, one rice, three side dishes (*okazu*) and a pickle. This is known as *ichi-ju sansai* ("1-1-3"). One side is a protein like egg, meat or fish; the others are vegetables or salads presented on several small plates. These veggie sides are prepared by simply steaming or boiling, and they are served with a dollop of savory sauce like our Green Veggies with Sesame Dressing (page 67).

Our Japanese Vegetable Fried Rice (page 72) combines left-over rice with a host of stir-fried veggies. Add shrimp or chicken and it is a meal on its own!

Press shapes from carrots and *daikon* radishes to top your salads. Then, spoon tangy Carrot Ginger Dressing (page 73) over the greens for a bonus veggie serving. A good diet includes two handfuls of vegetables per day. What a great way to add them in!

Vegetables & Fruit   65

Mottainai (What a Waste!)

Let's try these activities to avoid being wasteful (*mottainai*). Save leftover green onion bulbs and clementine peels and give them a new purpose!

Clementine Peels: Fresh and Dried

Tear peels of clementines into pieces and toss them into your bath to create a nice fragrance! (Don't let them go down the drain.) Or, lay torn skins on a paper towel to air-dry for a few days. Once dried, store in a jar. Drop a few pieces into hot tea or hot water for a citrusy sip. Drop a few pieces in sparkling water to give it the scent of clementine!

Grow a Green Onion

It's easy to grow your own green onion (scallion) from a leftover bulb—no waste from cooking! ☺

❶ Fill a very small cup or jar ¾ of the way full with water.

❷ Cut a green onion at about 2 in (5 cm) from the bottom, leaving the long roots on the bulb. Save the rest of the green onion to use for cooking.

❸ Place the green onion bulb root-side down in water, as shown in the photo. You can use a toothpick to help position the cutting in the container.

❹ Place the container on a sunny windowsill. In a few days' time, you will see it begin to grow! When ready to harvest, cut pieces to use in recipes.

Green Veggies with Sesame Dressing

This popular side dish (*okazu*) uses pre-roasted sesame seeds in the dressing. The sesame seeds are crushed to release more flavor and an aroma that makes you hungry!

Makes about 1½ cups (about 125 g)   **Prep time:** 15 minutes   **Cook time:** 5 minutes

INGREDIENTS

- 10 broccoli florets or ¼ lb (125 g) green beans, sliced in thirds on an angle
- 1 tablespoon soy sauce
- 1–2 teaspoons sugar
- 1 tablespoon water
- 1 tablespoon roasted sesame seeds (iri goma), crushed (see right)

METHOD

❶ Bring a half pot of salted water to a boil. Lower the heat and add the broccoli or green beans and cook for 3–5 minutes until just tender.

❷ Fill a mixing bowl halfway with cold water and a few ice cubes.

❸ Remove the vegetables with tongs and place them into the cold water to stop the cooking process and keep the vegetables green. Drain.

❹ In a separate bowl, combine the soy sauce, sugar and water. Mix until the sugar is dissolved.

❺ Crush the sesame seeds using one of the methods described in the following section. Once you smell their aroma, they are ready to use. Add them to the soy sauce mixture and mix well.

❻ Pour the dressing over the vegetables and toss until well coated.

THREE WAYS TO CRUSH SESAME SEEDS

- Use a Japanese mortar and pestle (*suribachi*) or standard white ceramic mortar and pestle to grind the sesame seeds—not too fine.
- Process the seeds in a food processor by pulsing a few times.
- Lay the roasted sesame seeds between 2 pieces of wax paper or parchment paper. Use a rolling pin or can to press and roll back and forth.

Vegetables & Fruit

Grape Tomato Hearts

Say "I ♥ you" with a tomato! Tuck grape tomato hearts in your lunch box or between two mini mozzarella cheese balls or any other veggie for a visual hug. The size and shape of the tomato will affect the final result—cherry tomatoes are too round for this application.

INGREDIENT
- One or 2 grape tomatoes

METHOD For one tomato:

1 Lay the grape tomato on a cutting board and, with a small serrated knife, cut the tomato in half on a diagonal.

2 Rotate one half of the tomato so the top halves meet in the middle. You now have a ♥.

3 Put a decorative or plain toothpick through the halves to keep them together.

METHOD For two tomatoes:

1 Lay a grape tomato on a cutting board.

2 On a diagonal, cut about a ½-in (1.25-cm) slice off the narrow end of the tomato. Do the same to the other tomato.

3 Slide the two tomatoes together so the narrow ends' flat sides meet. You have a ♥! Push a toothpick or skewer through the tomato halves to hold them together.

Clementine Juice Jelly Cups

Jello is popular in "*Okosama* Lunches"— special meals for kids in many restaurants in Japan. Make a refreshing gelatin from clementine juice. Make a natural bowl from the fruit, or use a small glass cup.

Makes about four ½-cup (125 ml) servings **Prep time:** 25 minutes **Cook time:** 3 minutes

INGREDIENTS

- 6–8 clementines, halved
- 4 whole clementines (for bowls) (optional)
- ½ cup (125 ml) boiling water
- 1 packet (0.25 oz) unflavored gelatin
- 2 tablespoons sugar
- 1 teaspoon freshly squeezed lemon juice
- Mint leaves, for garnish

METHOD

❶ Use a citrus juicer to squeeze approximately 1¼ cups (300 ml) of juice from the halved clementines. Don't throw away the skins! (See page 66.)

❷ For the bowls (if using): Cut off about ¼ of the tops of the whole clementines. With a spoon, carefully scoop out the fruit from each. Save a few fruit segments for decoration and use the rest for a snack.

❸ Place ¼ cup (65 ml) of the juice in a small saucepan. Sprinkle on the gelatin powder to start dissolving it.

❹ Add the boiled water and mix well until the gelatin is dissolved.

❺ Add the sugar and the remaining clementine juice, as well as the lemon juice. Heat the mixture over medium-low heat for about 2 minutes, stirring until the sugar is dissolved.

❻ Ladle the mixture into 4 cups or into the prepared clementine bowls. Refrigerate for at least 2 hours. Once the gelatin is set, decorate each portion with a reserved clementine segment and a mint leaf.

Vegetables & Fruit

Edible Decorations for Your Plate

Me de taberu is a Japanese saying that means "eat with your eyes." Feast on these colorful decorations for your plate or *bento* box—they are all edible! It is easy to make any meal more appetizing by adding decorations that you can eat. Make your own using mini vegetable cutters, cookie cutters, cute picks, small scissors and your creativity! Here are a few ideas to get you started.

Vegetable and Cookie Cutters

Vegetable cutter sets come in several sizes and designs, and are widely available online. For small children, cook carrot rounds in the microwave for about 30 seconds to make them easy to cut.

INGREDIENTS
- Red, green and yellow bell peppers
- Carrot and cucumber rounds
- Cheddar cheese slices

METHOD

❶ Cut pieces of vegetables, fruit and cheese to sizes with enough area for the cutters to work.

❷ Press a variety of shapes into the skin of the fruits and veggies. Use both the cutter shape and the perimeter of your edible "canvas" to create your decorations. Trim the perimeter to a square and set the same shape in a different color into the empty space.

Tip: when you punch out bell peppers with the shapes, press the cutter against the inside of the skin, not the shiny side. It will be easier to cut straight through. Trim the edges with small scissors.

Cucumber Coils

INGREDIENT
- 1 mini cucumber

METHOD

❶ Lay a cucumber on a cutting board, horizontally. Hold down the tip of the cucumber with a small fork.

❷ Take a vegetable peeler and, from the tip, pull the vegetable peeler across the cucumber. You will have a flat strip of cucumber peel. Repeat this another 2 or 3 times until you have several strips.

❸ Roll the strip into a coil. Use a toothpick to hold the roll together if necessary.

Radish Balls

INGREDIENT
- 1 radish

METHOD

❶ Cut 2 thin slices of radish.

❷ Lay them flat on the table.

❸ Find the center of one radish slice. With the tip of a knife, pierce the center and bring your knife straight down. This will make a slit. Repeat with the other radish slice.

❹ Slide one radish into the other through the slits, creating a "ball." Twist the slit edges slightly, making them offset.

Edamame Picks

METHOD

Spear several *edamame* together on a cool pick for easy handling.

Strawberry Hearts

INGREDIENT • 1 large strawberry

METHOD

❶ Remove the green stem of the strawberry.
❷ Cut the strawberry in half from top to bottom.
❸ Lay the strawberry halves flat side down on a cutting board.
❹ Make a V-shaped notch at the top of the strawberry with the tip of a knife.

Tomato Roses

You will need the help of an adult to create one continuous strip of tomato skin. Then you can wind it into the shape of a rose.

INGREDIENT • 1 small tomato (Campari size)

METHOD

❶ Place the tomato on a cutting board, stem end up. With a small paring knife, starting at the stem end of the tomato, slip the knife under the skin and carefully slice only the skin away from the tomato while continually turning the tomato. Try not to break the strip. If you do, don't worry; you can still use all the pieces.
❷ Wind the strip around your finger and then place it down on the cutting board. Carefully turn it over. You have a tomato rose!

Vegetables & Fruit 71

Japanese Vegetable Fried Rice (Chahan)

Originally from China, this Japanese-style fried rice is popular in households all over Japan. It is a great dish that allows you to mix small amounts of leftover meat and vegetables with rice. Use rice that has been in the fridge for a day. This dries it out, making it easier to pan fry. Use a colorful mix of vegetables with a variety of textures. Cut vegetables to about the same size so they are all done cooking at the same time. Add any protein you like.

Serves 4–6
Prep time: 25 minutes
Cook time: 10 mins (excludes rice)

INGREDIENTS

- 1½ tablespoons canola oil or sesame oil, divided
- 2 green onions (scallions), trimmed, white and green parts, sliced into thin rings
- 1 carrot, cut into ½-in (1.25-cm) dice
- 2 stalks celery, cut into ½-in (1.25-cm) dice
- 5 fresh shiitake mushrooms (or other mushrooms), cut in thin slices
- ½ teaspoon salt
- 3 cups (600 g) cooked Japanese rice (see pages 26–27), cold
- 1–2 tablespoons soy sauce
- 1 egg, beaten
- ½ cup (65 g) fresh or frozen green peas
- Salt and pepper, to taste

METHOD

1 Heat 1 tablespoon of the oil in a large skillet over medium heat. Add the green onions, carrots, celery and *shiitake* mushrooms. Sprinkle on the salt. Stir-fry the vegetables for about 2 minutes, or until the carrots are cooked but still firm. (If you are adding protein, this is the time to do it. Cook bite-size pieces of chicken or shrimp for another 2 minutes, or until the flesh has turned white.)

2 Add the rice and, with a spatula, press it into the skillet as you mix it with the vegetables. Cook for about 3 minutes, until the rice gets a little crunchy.

3 Add the soy sauce and mix until well combined.

4 With the spatula, push the rice mixture to one side of the pan. In the empty area, add the remaining oil, and then the egg. Scramble the egg for about 1 minute, and then mix it with the rice.

5 Add the peas and cook for 1 minute. Adjust seasoning, to taste.

NOTE Frozen mixed vegetables can be used.

Carrot Ginger Dressing

This tangy and nutritious dressing was inspired by Namiko Hirasawa Chen from "Just One Cookbook," a wildly popular website for Japanese cooking. The great thing about it is that you have added another vegetable to your salad just by pouring it over your greens. Prepare it in a blender or grate the carrot and ginger on the small holes of a box grater.

Makes ½ cup (125 ml)
Prep time: 15 minutes

INGREDIENTS

- 1 carrot, peeled
- ½- to 1-in (1.25- to 2.5-cm) piece fresh ginger, peeled
- ¼ cup (65 ml) rice vinegar
- 3 tablespoons oil
- 1 tablespoon sugar
- ¼ teaspoon salt

FOR THE SALAD

- 2 cups (100 g) mixed lettuce leaves
- 3-in (7.5-cm) piece daikon radish, peeled

METHOD

1. Cut the carrot into 3 or 4 pieces and place in a blender.
2. Cut the ginger into 3 pieces and add it to the blender.
3. Add the vinegar, oil, sugar and salt. Cover the blender and blend for about 1 minute, until the dressing is smooth. Blend more if necessary. It's okay if the dressing is not perfectly smooth. Pour the dressing into a jar and keep in the refrigerator.
4. To Serve: Prepare the lettuce and place it in a serving bowl.
5. Cut out fun shapes from the *daikon* radish using mini cookie or veggie cutters.
6. Spoon the dressing over the salad. Decorate with the *daikon* cut outs.

TIP
How to Peel Ginger
Scrape the back of a spoon over the skin of a piece of ginger. The brown skin will easily flake away.

Vegetables & Fruit   73

Fruit Sandos

Is it a sandwich? Is it dessert? It's the unique Japanese Fruit Sando! Slightly sweetened whipped cream is spread on white bread topped with fruit laid out to form special patterns when cut. This simple layout makes circles when cut, but you can get creative and combine different fruits and make your own design! Choose a variety of soft, healthy fruits for pops of color. Firm fruits like apples and pears are not suitable.

Makes 4 sandwiches
Prep time: 35 minutes

INGREDIENTS

- 2 cups (500 ml) unsweetened heavy or whipping cream
- ¼ cup (28 g) powdered sugar
- 1 teaspoon vanilla extract
- 8 slices firm white bread or Japanese milk bread (shoku pan)
- 6 strawberries, rinsed and dried
- 2 clementines
- 2 kiwis
- 1 banana

METHOD

1 Place a large mixing bowl and 2 beaters in the refrigerator for 20 minutes. Add the heavy cream, powdered sugar and vanilla extract to the mixing bowl. Beat on medium speed until the whipped cream is stiff and holds a peak. Cover with plastic wrap and chill until ready to use.

2 Have a large plate on hand. Prepare the fruit: Remove the stems from the strawberries, peel the skin from the kiwis and clementines. (Save the clementine skins: see page 66.)

3 Peel the banana just prior to use.

④ For each sandwich, lay out a 10-in (20-cm) piece of plastic wrap on a cutting board. Set 1 piece of bread on top.

⑤ Spread a thick layer of whipped cream on one slice of bread. Refer to the photos above for the placement of the fruit on each slice of bread, so when you make vertical cuts in step ⑧, you will reveal cross-sections of the fruit. Note: WHOLE strawberries are placed down the middle.

⑥ Spread another layer of whipped cream on top of the fruit. Then, top with a second piece of bread.

⑦ Fold the plastic wrap firmly around the sandwich. Repeat this process to make the remaining sandwiches. Place the sandwiches in the refrigerator for at least 30 minutes before cutting.

⑧ Take a sharp knife and carefully swipe both sides of the blade with a wet paper towel. Place a sandwich on the cutting board. **Do not remove the plastic wrap**. Starting at the top of the sandwich, slowly make a vertical cut with a seesaw motion, cutting through the fruit from top to bottom. Separate the halves, unwrap and place on a plate, fruit-side up.

Vegetables & Fruit 75

CHAPTER 5

JAPANESE FAVORITES

B級グルメ

Pizza! Hot dogs! Hamburgers! Tacos! Ramen! Everyone recognizes and loves these foods, and all of them have found a home in Japan! Because traditional ingredients are not available everywhere, and because local preferences are unique, the adopted recipes have been fine-tuned to suit the Japanese palate and pantry.

Some popular foods can be high in salt, sugar and fat. While it is okay to have these foods occasionally, having the right amount is good. It's wise to learn to read a nutrition label so you know what—and how much of it—is in your food.

The recipes in this chapter use more vegetables and less salt. Both of the ramens have fresh ginger, garlic and *miso* to pump up the flavor. Our Japanese Savory Pancakes are stuffed with shredded cabbage and carrot strips to add crunch and fiber. The top is decorated with a special sauce and some mayonnaise in a cool pattern! There are equal portions of veggies and meat in our Pot Stickers, adding flavor and texture. And our Kid's Lunch Special hits all the right notes, with a variety of foods in small portions. As you learn to cook, you'll learn how you can make your own recipes healthier too!

Okosama Lunch–Kid's Lunch Special

"*Okosama* lunch" is a special kid's menu at restaurants in Japan (*okosama* is a polite way to say "child"). Often, the choices are based on Western-style food with a Japanese twist. Rice with ketchup is shaped to look like Mt. Fuji and the plates and presentation are designed to bring a big smile to a kid's face. There is even a little prize! This retro bullet train plate was given to Debra's son, Brad, when he was 3 and the family lived in Japan. "He loved going out for *Okosama* lunch. Now Brad's son, my grandson, enjoys using the same awesome plate!"

Ketchup Rice

Add ketchup to white rice for color and flavor.

Makes 1 serving **Prep time:** 10 minutes
Cook time: n/a (excludes making the rice)

INGREDIENTS

- ½ cup (100 g) cooked Japanese rice (see pages 26–27)
- 2 teaspoons ketchup
- ½ teaspoon Simple Nori Furikake (see page 43) (optional)

METHOD

❶ Mix the warm rice and ketchup in a small bowl.

❷ Rub the inside of a small custard cup with a wet paper towel. Add the rice and press lightly. Put a small plate on top of the cup and flip the cup and plate over together. Holding the cup carefully, gently shake the molded rice from the cup.

❸ Place a spatula under the rice and slide it onto the main serving plate. Top with the furikake, (if using).

Steamed Broccoli with Lemon Juice and Soy Sauce

The super-simple dressing elevates the broccoli with a savory-citrus pop of flavor.

Makes 1 serving **Prep time:** 5 minutes
Cook time: 5 minutes

INGREDIENTS

- Pinch of salt
- 5 broccoli florets, rinsed
- ½ teaspoon soy sauce
- ¼ teaspoon freshly squeezed lemon juice

METHOD

❶ Fill a small saucepan halfway with water. Add the salt. Heat the water on moderately high heat until it begins to boil.

❷ Add the broccoli florets and reduce the heat to medium. Cover the pan. Cook for 2 minutes. The broccoli should be bright green.

❸ With tongs, remove the broccoli from the pan and place it in a bowl. Sprinkle on the soy sauce and lemon juice. Serve at room temperature.

Clementine Juice Jelly Cup
See page 69

Fruit jelly is a refreshing dessert after a meal. We use a hollowed out clementine as a bowl to hold the gelatin dessert. It makes a great presentation topped with a mint leaf or any fruit of your choosing. No time to whip up jello? Simply cut the clementine in half and carefully remove the segments. Put the segments back into your clementine "bowl" and top with a mint leaf for a cool presentation.

Yakult Drink

Yakult is a popular sweetened fermented milk drink that has the same "good bacteria" as yogurt. It was invented in Japan. "Yakult Ladies" used to sell this drink door to door on a bicycle—in some countries they still do! This drink has become popular around the world.

Japanese Favorites 79

Corn Potage

This velvety corn soup is easy-to-make and can be served warm or cold. "A sprinkling of salt brings out the natural sweetness of the corn," says Wa-Sho instructor, Yoko Ho.

Makes Four ½-cup (125 ml) servings
Prep time: 5 minutes **Cook time:** 10 minutes

INGREDIENTS

- 1 green onion (scallion), trimmed
- 1 tablespoon butter
- 1 cup (150 g) canned or frozen corn kernels, thawed
- ½ teaspoon soy sauce
- 1¼ cups (300 ml) milk
- ¼ teaspoon salt, plus more, to taste

METHOD

❶ Thinly slice the green onion. Keep the white and green parts separated.

❷ Melt the butter in a small saucepan over medium heat. Add the white part of the green onion slices and stir-fry for 1 minute.

❸ Set a tablespoon of corn kernels aside. Add the remaining corn and mix until coated with the butter. Cook for 1 minute. Add the soy sauce.

❹ Add the milk and heat over medium low heat for 2–3 minutes. Turn off the heat. Let the soup cool (this is important!) for about 5 minutes.

❺ Once the soup has cooled, pour it into a blender. Add the ¼ teaspoon of salt. Blend for about 1 minute. Taste and adjust the seasoning.

❻ Re-heat over low heat, if serving warm. Serve in small cups and top with the reserved corn kernels and green part of the green onion slices.

Teriyaki Chicken Meatballs

Pair Teriyaki Sauce (page 60) with meatballs, and you have a winning combination!

Makes About 16 meatballs
Prep time: 10 minutes **Cook time:** 10 minutes

INGREDIENTS

- 1 lb (500 g) ground chicken (or beef)
- 1 clove garlic, finely chopped
- 1-in (2.5-cm) piece fresh ginger, peeled and grated
- 1 teaspoon soy sauce
- ½ cup (60 g) cornstarch
- ¼ cup (65 ml) Teriyaki Sauce (see page 60)

METHOD

❶ Add the ground chicken (or beef), garlic, ginger and soy sauce to a mixing bowl.

❷ Spread the cornstarch onto a plate.

❸ In a medium saucepan over medium heat, bring about 4 cups (1 liter) of water to a boil. Then, lower the heat to a simmer.

❹ With a soup spoon, scoop about 1½ tablespoon portions of the meat mixture, roll each into balls, and coat them in the cornstarch.

❺ Bring the water back to a boil. Carefully drop half of the meat balls into the boiling water. They will rise to the top and float. Lower the heat to medium low and cook for 3 more minutes. Transfer the cooked meatballs to a clean plate using a slotted spoon. Repeat this step to cook the remaining meatballs.

❻ Pour the Teriyaki Sauce into a small skillet. Bring the sauce to a simmer over low heat. Add the meatballs and gently toss them in the sauce to coat. Cook for one minute. Move them to a plate. Cool before putting 2 or 3 on a skewer.

Learn How to Read a Nutrition Label

Most foods are good to eat sometimes, but balance is key! Some foods are more nutritious than others. This is where reading the list of ingredients and understanding food labels come in handy. The numbers on the label are in relation to the recommended amount for your body to have for an entire day.

Pay attention to Saturated Fat, Trans Fat, Sodium and Added Sugars!

These are the items on a label where the lower the number, the healthier the food will generally be.

1. Servings
2. Calories
3. Fats
4. Sodium
5. Added Sugars
6. Micronutrients
7. Footnote

Nutrition Facts
8 servings per container
Serving size 2/3 cup (55g)

Amount per serving
Calories 230

	% Daily Value*
Total Fat 8g	10%
Saturated Fat 1g	5%
Trans Fat 0g	
Cholesterol 0mg	0%
Sodium 160mg	7%
Total Carbohydrate 37g	13%
Dietary Fiber 4g	14%
Total Sugars 12g	
Includes 10g Added Sugars	20%
Protein 3g	
Vitamin D 2mcg	10%
Calcium 260mg	20%
Iron 8mg	45%
Potassium 235mg	6%

* The % Daily Value (DV) tells you how much a serving of food contributes to a daily diet. 2,000 calories a day is used for general nutrition advice.

Amount (out of 100) of the recommended daily maximum allowance

Avoid overconsumption of these nutrients

Japanese Favorites 81

Ramen

Ramen is a nest of noodles in a flavorful broth with toppings that can include vegetables, pork, egg and seaweed. It is one of the most recognizable Japanese dishes with Chinese origins. The simple broth is packed with lots of seasonings and healthier than the packaged version.

Shoyu (Soy Sauce) Ramen

Even though this is soy-sauce flavored ramen, we use a small amount of *miso* for added flavor. To save energy, clean-up time and nutrients, we cook the veggies and ramen in the same water. Slices of chicken breast, pork, beef or tofu can also be added to the toppings for a protein boost.

Serves 2–4   **Prep time:** 15 minutes   **Cook time:** 15 minutes

PREPARE THE BROTH, VEGGIES AND NOODLES

INGREDIENTS

- 4 cups (1 liter) low-sodium beef, chicken or vegetable broth
- 1 tablespoon miso paste
- 1 tablespoon soy sauce
- 1 teaspoon sugar
- 1 teaspoon dark sesame oil, plus more, for drizzling
- 2 cloves garlic, finely chopped
- 3 thin slices fresh ginger, peeled and finely chopped
- Salt and pepper, to taste, plus more salt, for sprinkling
- 6 cups (1.5 liters) water
- One 10-oz (285-g) package fresh spinach
- 8 oz (250 g) fresh bean sprouts
- 1 lb (500 g) fresh or dried ramen noodles

METHOD

❶ In a medium saucepan over medium heat, add the beef, chicken or vegetable broth.

❷ When broth is hot, add the *miso* paste, soy sauce, sugar, sesame oil, garlic, ginger, salt and pepper. Simmer for 2 minutes. Turn off the heat.

❸ In a separate large saucepan over high heat, bring 6 cups (1.5 liters) of water to a boil.

❹ Add the spinach. Lower heat and cook for 1 minute. With a pair of tongs, remove the spinach, place in a strainer and press out the liquid. Do not throw out the cooking liquid! Place on a plate and sprinkle with a pinch of salt.

❺ Bring the water back to a boil. Add the beansprouts and cook for 1 minute. Remove with tongs to the strainer and place the sprouts in a bowl. Drizzle with sesame oil and sprinkle with a pinch of salt.

❻ Add more water if necessary to cook the noodles. Bring back to a boil. Cook the noodles according to directions on the package. With a pair of tongs, remove the noodles to a strainer.

82   Chapter 5

TIP
Ramen/noodle etiquette: In Japan it is POLITE TO SLURP and make noise while you are eating noodles. It cools down the noodles and the sound means you are enjoying your meal!

ASSEMBLE THE BOWLS

ADDITIONAL TOPPINGS

- 2–4 plain hard-boiled or Ramen Eggs (page 86), peeled
- 1 cup (150 g) canned or frozen corn kernels, thawed
- Four 2-in (5-cm) nori (roasted seaweed) strips
- 1 green onion (scallion), trimmed and finely sliced (optional)
- Spicy chili oil—rayu (optional)

METHOD

❶ Heat the broth over medium heat until it begins to simmer. Taste and adjust seasonings.

❷ If the noodles have gotten sticky, loosen them with a little warm water. Using tongs, divide the noodles into 4 bowls.

❸ Cut the boiled eggs in half.

❹ Ladle hot broth over the noodles.

❺ Divide the toppings, including the spinach and bean sprouts, placing each ingredient in a small pile on top of the noodles. Sprinkle on the green onions, if using. Drizzle on the spicy oil, if using.

❻ Serve with a spoon and chopsticks. Use your dominant hand to hold the chopsticks and your other hand to hold the spoon. Dip the spoon into the broth and use the chopsticks to pick up the noodles and toppings.

Japanese Favorites 83

Miso Ramen

Everyone loves ramen in Japan and now everywhere in the world! Each region has their own special ramen. In Hokkaido, the northern island, the soup base is made with *miso* paste. We use ground pork, but you could use ground chicken or crumbled tofu. It makes the soup very tasty. To add some zip to your ramen bowl, add a dash of chili oil (*rayu*). It's fun to dress up the top of the ramen with curly green onion slivers.

Serves 2–4   **Prep time:** 15 minutes   **Cook time:** 15 minutes

INGREDIENTS

- 2–4 plain hard-boiled eggs or Ramen Eggs (see page 86), peeled
- 2 green onions (scallions), trimmed, white parts only
- 2 cloves garlic, finely chopped
- 3 thin slices fresh ginger, peeled and finely chopped
- 1 tablespoon soy sauce
- 1 teaspoon sugar
- 1 teaspoon sesame oil
- 3–4 tablespoons miso paste (any type is fine—the darker, the saltier and stronger the flavor)
- 1 tablespoon canola oil
- 8 oz (250 g) ground pork (or chicken, turkey, beef or drained and crumbled firm tofu)
- 8 oz (250 g) fresh bean sprouts
- 1 cup (150 g) canned or frozen corn kernels, thawed
- 4 cups (1 liter) water
- Salt and pepper, to taste
- 1 lb (450 g) fresh or dry ramen noodles
- Four 2-in (5-cm) nori (roasted seaweed) strips
- Spicy chili oil—rayu (optional)

METHOD

❶ Cut the boiled eggs in half. Set aside.

❷ Prepare a bowl of cold water with ice cubes. Cut the green onion pieces in half lengthwise. Place flat side down on a cutting board. With the tip of a knife, starting at the top of each piece, slice the green onion straight down to the bottom in thin slivers. Place the green onion slivers into the bowl of ice water. Set aside. They will curl up in minutes.

❸ Place the garlic and ginger in a small mixing bowl. Add the soy sauce, sugar, sesame oil and *miso*. These are your seasonings. Mix well and set aside.

❹ In a large saucepan, add the canola oil and heat over medium heat. Add the ground pork, beansprouts and corn. Stir-fry until the pork is no longer pink and the beansprouts have wilted.

❺ Add the water to the pork mixture. Over medium heat, bring the mixture to a simmer. Continue cooking on low for about 3 minutes. Add the *miso*-sauce seasoning mixture and stir until completely dissolved. You may need to add a little more water if the mixture is too thick. Taste and add salt and pepper, if needed. Turn off the heat.

❻ In another large saucepan, bring 8 cups (1.75 liters) of water to a boil. Add the noodles and cook according to package directions. If you are using fresh noodles, pay attention to the cooking time—it is very short! Pour the noodles into a strainer.

❼ Remove green onion slivers from the ice water and place them on a paper towel to drain.

❽ To serve: With tongs, divide the ramen among 2 large, or 4 smaller, bowls. Ladle out just the broth and add it to ramen bowls. Spoon the pork and vegetable mixture on top of the noodles. Top each bowl with 1 or 2 hard-boiled egg halves, a piece of *nori* and green onion slivers. Drizzle on the spicy oil, if using.

❾ Serve with a spoon and chopsticks. Use your dominant hand to hold the chopsticks and your other hand to hold the spoon. Dip the spoon into the broth and use the chopsticks to pick up the noodles and toppings.

Japanese Favorites

Ramen Eggs–Soy Sauce Seasoned Boiled Eggs (Ajitsuke Tamago)

These famous "ramen eggs" are bathed in seasonings to absorb delicious flavors. They are popular in *bento* boxes and for picnics. The yolk is usually soft, but cook the egg to your liking. Keep the eggs in contact with the marinade for even seasoning.

Makes 2 eggs
Prep time: 5 minutes, plus 1–12 hours to marinate
Cook time: 7 minutes

INGREDIENTS

- 2 eggs
- 1 tablespoon soy sauce
- 1 teaspoon sugar
- 1 teaspoon mirin
- 1 tablespoon water

METHOD

❶ Fill a small saucepan ¾ full with water. On high heat, bring to a boil, and then lower the heat to medium.

❷ Use a spoon to carefully lower the eggs it into the boiling water.

❸ For a soft yolk, cook for 7 minutes. For a firmer yolk, cook for 9 minutes.

❹ Remove the eggs with a slotted spoon and place them in a bowl of ice water.

❺ Peel the boiled eggs and place them in a zip-top plastic bag.

❻ Mix the soy sauce, sugar, *mirin* and water in a bowl until the sugar has dissolved.

❼ Pour the mixture over the eggs and seal the bag. Roll the eggs around in the mixture to coat them. You can also use a small container with a tight-fitting lid.

❽ Marinate for between 1 hour to overnight in the refrigerator. Gently shake the container a couple of times to move the eggs around in the marinade.

❾ Remove the eggs and discard the liquid. Cut them in half and serve them on top of ramen.

TIP
Find a tall glass to put the bag with the eggs and seasoning mixture into. The eggs will stack, with the liquid surrounding them.

Kid's Special Stir-fried Udon Noodles
(Yaki Udon)

Ramen noodles are so popular, but have you tried chewy *udon* noodles? With lots of veggies and mini hot dogs, this is popular! You can find *udon* noodles fresh or frozen, or dried like pasta in a long package. To season, use Easy Homemade Okonomiyaki Sauce (page 89), or sprinkle on soy sauce.

Serves 1–2 **Prep time:** 15 minutes **Cook time:** 15 minutes

INGREDIENTS

- 1 tablespoon oil
- ¼ medium-size cabbage, cut into 1-in (2.5-cm) pieces
- 1 carrot, cut into thin matchsticks
- 2 green onions (scallions), trimmed and sliced on the diagonal
- ¼ teaspoon salt
- 5 mini hot dogs (cocktail franks), cut in half on the diagonal, or 2 hot dogs, cut in 5 pieces, each on the diagonal (or pieces of chicken or ham)
- 2 tablespoons water
- One 7-oz (200-g) packet of fresh or frozen udon noodles
- 2–3 tablespoons homemade (see page 89) or bottled okonomiyaki sauce, or soy sauce

METHOD

❶ Add the oil to a large skillet and heat over medium heat. Add the cabbage, carrot and green onions, and sprinkle on the salt.

❷ Use tongs to stir fry the vegetables for about 2 minutes, until they begin to soften.

❸ Add the mini hot dogs, and continue to cook over medium heat for another 2 minutes.

❹ Add the water and cook for another minute.

❺ Place fresh noodles directly into the skillet and mix with the vegetables. They will begin to loosen as you fry them. (If using dried noodles, cook separately according to the package directions. If using frozen noodles, cook for one minute in boiling water and drain.)

❻ Add the *okonomiyaki* sauce or soy sauce to the noodles and toss until well mixed. Taste and adjust seasoning.

Japanese Favorites

Japanese Savory Pancakes (Okonomiyaki)

Okonomi means "as you like it" and *yaki* means "to grill or fry." It is a type of food called *yoshoku*—Western-style food that has been adopted and is now so popular in Japan. This pancake can include, shrimp, bacon, strips of pork or chicken—with lots of veggies, as you like! *Okonomiyaki* restaurants are famous for their tabletop griddles, where the pancake is made right in front of you and you can choose your toppings. Try an *okonomiyaki* party at home with your friends and family.

Makes Two 6-in (15-cm) pancakes
Serves about 4 **Prep time:** 25 minutes **Cook time:** 15 minutes

INGREDIENTS

BATTER
- 1 cup (150 g) flour
- ½ teaspoon salt
- ½ cup (125 ml) water—or more if needed
- 2 eggs

FILLING
- 2 cups (250 g) shredded green cabbage (about ¼ medium head) or 1 package coleslaw mix (pre-cut cabbage)
- 1 carrot, shredded
- ½ red bell pepper, deseeded and thinly sliced
- 4 green onions (scallions), trimmed, cut in thirds and sliced lengthwise
- 2 tablespoons oil
- 2–3 slices bacon, cut in half (or slices of baked ham, 1 cup / 155 g shredded cooked chicken, or 10 raw shrimp)
- Easy Homemade Okonomiyaki Sauce (see recipe, opposite), or store-bought
- 2 tablespoons Kewpie mayonnaise, or any other mayonnaise brand (optional)

ADDITIONAL OPTIONAL TOPPINGS:
- Seaweed flakes – *aonori*
- Bonito fish flakes
- Green onion (scallion) slices (green parts)

METHOD

❶ Combine the flour, salt, water and eggs in a mixing bowl. Whisk together until well combined.

❷ Add the cabbage, carrot, red bell pepper and green onions to the batter. Gently fold in the vegetables until well combined.

❸ Preheat a large skillet over medium heat, or use an electric griddle. Add the oil and heat for 30 seconds. Add half of the batter, making a 6-in (15-cm) circle. Lay half of the bacon over the uncooked batter. Fry for about 3 minutes, until the bottom begins to brown.

Easy Homemade Okonomiyaki Sauce

Use this sauce for *okonomiyaki*, for dipping fried Tofu Croquettes (page 62) or for Kids Special Stir-fried Udon Noodles (page 87).

Makes ⅓ cup (80 ml)

INGREDIENTS

- 4 tablespoons ketchup
- 1 tablespoon Worcestershire sauce, or more, to taste
- 2 tablespoons grated apple or apple juice

METHOD

❶ Combine all of the ingredients in a medium size bowl, and mix well. It's ready to use!

❹ Use 1 or 2 spatulas to flip the pancake. Cook for 4 minutes.

❺ Flip again and cook for an additional 3 minutes. Cut into the center with the tip of your knife to make sure the batter is cooked.

❻ Place the pancake on a plate or cutting board. Spread the sauce over the top in a zigzag or spiral design. If using mayonnaise from a plastic bottle, make lines in the opposite direction. Then, take a toothpick and pull it straight through the mayonnaise to create a marbleized design.

❼ Cut in a grid, or slice like a pizza! Sprinkle on seaweed, bonito flakes or green onions, if using.

Japanese Favorites   89

Pot Stickers (Gyoza)

Gyoza, or pot stickers, are dumplings. Many cultures have their own special dumplings, such as *mandu* from Korea, or tortellini from Italy. Japanese gyoza are based on the Chinese dumpling, *jiaozi*. The shape resembles a gold ingot, which represents good fortune.

Makes about 30 pot stickers   **Prep time:** 45 minutes   **Cook time:** 10 minutes

INGREDIENTS

FILLING
- ¼ Napa cabbage (about 14 oz / 400 g), or green cabbage, cored and coarsely chopped (yields about 1½ cups)
- 1½ teaspoons salt, divided
- 8 oz (225 g) ground pork (or chicken, or turkey) or ½ block of firm tofu drained well and crumbled (see page 105)
- 2 green onions (scallions), trimmed and minced
- 1 carrot, grated (optional)
- 1-in (2.5-cm) piece fresh ginger (peeled and grated)
- 2 cloves garlic, minced
- 1 tablespoon soy sauce
- 2 teaspoons sesame oil
- 30 gyoza wrappers (or more)
- 2 tablespoons canola oil, for frying

DIPPING SAUCE
- 2 tablespoons soy sauce
- 2 teaspoons rice vinegar

90   Chapter 5

METHOD

1 In a large bowl, add the coarsely chopped cabbage and sprinkle with 1 teaspoon of the salt. Set aside for 5 minutes. Over the sink, squeeze out the water with your hands. Finely chop the cabbage and place it in a large bowl.

2 Add the ground meat or tofu, and the green onions and carrots, if using. Mix well.

3 Add the ginger, garlic, soy sauce and sesame oil. Add the remaining salt. Mix until combined.

4 Assemble the dumplings (see photos, at right). Prepare ½ cup of hot water.

5 In a large skillet with a cover, add the oil and heat over medium heat for 30 seconds. Add enough gyoza, to fill the pan in a single layer, flat-side down. Fry for 2 minutes or until the bottoms turn brown.

6 Slowly pour the hot water into the pan. Be careful—the hot oil could splatter! Cover and cook on medium-high heat for about 5 minutes, or until the water has evaporated.

7 Remove the cover and continue cooking as needed.

8 Transfer the gyoza to a large plate using a spatula.

9 Combine the soy sauce and vinegar in a small bowl and serve.

How to make the dumplings

METHOD

1 Place a wrapper in your palm or on a plate. Add a heaping teaspoon of the meat mixture into the center of the wrapper. Dip your index finger into water and trace around the edge of the wrapper.

2 Fold the bottom half over the filling onto the top of the gyoza wrapper. Press together. You now have a half-moon dumpling.

3 With 2 fingers, pinch a small section of the edge of the dumpling together. This makes a pleat. Do this 1 or 2 more times.

4 Press the dumpling into your palm to make a flat bottom. Or make your own shape!

5 Place on a floured baking sheet, flat side down. Repeat!

TIP
Freeze gyoza! Place the uncooked dumplings uncovered on a cookie sheet in the freezer until frozen. Transfer to a plastic bag. Do not defrost, cook according to the recipe. It may take a minute or two longer to cook.

Japanese Favorites

Teddy Bear Chicken and Veggie Omurice

Sometimes kids and parents love to make cute characters for mealtime fun! The popular teddy bear is molded from warm mixed rice. Two omelets make a pillow and tasty blanket. Follow the photos to learn how to create your own edible Teddy!

Makes 1 Teddy Bear (serves 2) **Prep time:** 30 minutes **Cook time:** 10 minutes (excludes making the rice)

INGREDIENTS

- 3 cups (approx. 600 g) cooked Japanese rice (see pages 26–27), warm
- 2 tablespoons ketchup, plus more for decoration
- 5 teaspoons canola oil, divided
- ½ small onion, diced
- 1 boneless, skinless chicken thigh, cut into 1-in (2.5-cm) pieces (or one 1-in / 2.5-cm thick slice of baked ham, diced)
- ¼ cup (about 80 g) mixed cooked fresh or frozen vegetables (corn, peas and carrots)
- 1 teaspoon soy sauce
- 3 eggs, divided
- 2 teaspoons sugar
- Dash of salt
- 1 teaspoon cornstarch
- 2 tablespoons water
- 1 slice cheddar cheese (for the features)
- ¼ sheet nori (roasted seaweed)

METHOD

RICE BALLS FOR THE TEDDY BEAR

❶ Place the warm rice in a bowl. Add the ketchup and mix well.

❷ Measure 1½ cups (300 g) of the ketchup rice and place it in a separate bowl. Use the following amounts to mold the head, ears and paws by twisting plastic wrap around the rice to create the shapes. Refer to the photo.

Head: ½ cup of rice

Ears: 2 tablespoons each of rice

Paws: the remaining rice

❸ In a medium skillet, add 3 teaspoons of the oil and stir-fry the onions for 2 minutes. Add the chicken and cook, stirring occasionally, until done, about 3 minutes. Add the vegetables, stir, and cook for another minute. Sprinkle on the soy sauce.

❹ Fold in the cooked chicken mixture to the bowl of remaining ketchup rice. Use the amounts of rice indicated below and plastic wrap to mold pillow and tummy.

Pillow: a few tablespoons of the chicken rice.

Tummy: the rest of the chicken rice.

OMELETS FOR PILLOW AND BLANKET

❶ In a small bowl beat the eggs. Add sugar and salt and mix well.

❷ Mix the cornstarch and water in a separate bowl. Add to the eggs. Mix well.

❸ Add 1 teaspoon of the oil to a small non-stick skillet over medium heat and heat for 30 seconds.

❹ **Pillow:** Pour about 3 tablespoons of the egg mixture into the skillet. Tip the pan so the egg makes a circle. Cook for 1 minute and turn off the heat. Turn the egg out onto a separate plate. Take the chicken rice that you set aside for the

pillow and place it in the center of the circle. Fold the egg around the rice and turn it over.

5 **Blanket**: Heat the skillet again and add the remaining oil. Pour the remaining eggs into the pan and, over medium low heat, tip the egg into a circle. Cook until just set. Turn off the heat and turn the egg out onto a plate.

PUT IT TOGETHER!

1 Unwrap the rice balls.

2 Place the pillow under part of the head. Place the ears on top, on either side of the head.

3 Place the blanket over the tummy. Trim the edges with scissors.

4 Place the paws on either side of the head above the blanket.

5 Cut the cheese into ears and a muzzle. Refer to the picture.

6 Cut 2 wide, U-shaped "sleeping eyes" and a small nose from the *nori*. Place them on the face.

7 Drizzle ketchup onto the blanket, and the Teddy Bear is done! Eat with a spoon!

Japanese Favorites 93

Kansha—Gratitude (感謝)

The Japanese term *Kansha* describes sincere appreciation and gratitude.

When eating, there are two forms of *kansha* that Japanese children use daily.

Itadakimasu—This is a term used at the beginning of every meal. It means "I humbly receive." You show gratitude to the foods—animals and plants—that were harvested, as well as to all the people who were involved in preparing the food.

Gochisosama Deshita—This term is used at the end of meals and means, "You worked hard preparing a delicious meal." It also shows gratitude for the food and to the person who made the meal, as well as those who grew and cultivated the food you enjoyed.

CHAPTER 6

SCHOOL LUNCHES

学校給食

Did you know that Japanese elementary school students have lunch in their classrooms with their teachers? Lunch is prepared fresh daily for each school and all children get the same meal. Students from first grade through sixth grade are responsible for serving the lunch to their classmates, and afterwards they clean up thoroughly, including wiping down tables and sweeping up any mess from the floors! Each day, several students are chosen to be the "food captains." They put on white jackets, cover their hair, put on gloves and are given their assignments. When the meal is done the captains load up a cart with the empty dishes and return it to the kitchen. During the lunch hour, the students also learn the importance of washing their hands, brushing their teeth and the proper use of chopsticks. These daily habits are a major part of their education.

    Japanese students learn to respect those who prepared and cleaned up after their meals and savor the food because it is fresh and delicious.

School Lunches (Kyushoku)

During the summers, Mayumi's family returns to Japan to visit, and her children go to the local elementary school. Her son has remarked, "The lunches are really good and healthy. I like that it is served by my classmates. I'm always excited to eat the delicious *kyushoku*."

Nikujaga- Japanese style Beef and Veggie Stew

This stew is a staple in Japanese households and schools. Thinly sliced meat, like shaved steak is used. To make this a Japanese school lunch experience, give each diner a tray with 3 dishes. Each person comes up to be served a portion of each dish.

Serves 4 **Prep time:** 20 minutes **Cook time:** 20 minutes

INGREDIENTS

- 15 snow pea pods, stringed, or ¼ cup (32 g) green peas
- 2 carrots
- 2 russet potatoes
- 1 large yellow onion
- 3 tablespoons sugar
- ½ teaspoon salt
- 3 tablespoons soy sauce
- 2 tablespoons mirin
- 2 tablespoons oil
- ½ lb (250 g) shaved steak or thinly sliced sirloin steak
- 1 cup (250 ml) water, or more if needed
- One 8-oz (250-g) packet shirataki* (or rice stick, or bean thread) noodles

Shirataki noodles are clear, chewy noodles made from a type of yam or tofu. You can find them in the refrigerated sections of many supermarkets.

METHOD

1. Cut parchment paper into a circle to fit inside your medium-size saucepan or skillet. It will be used as a "drop lid," to let the ingredients absorb the liquid and become more flavorful. Set it aside.

2. Cut the pea pods diagonally into 2–3 pieces.

3. Cut the carrots diagonally into 1-in (2.5-cm) pieces.

4. Peel the potatoes and cut them in half. Set the flat sides on the cutting board and cut the halves into 2-in (5-cm) chunks. Place them into a bowl of water to prevent them from turning brown.

5. Trim the onion and cut it in half from top to bottom. Set the flat sides on the cutting board and cut the halves into strips.

6. Mix the sugar, salt, soy sauce and *mirin* in a small bowl. Set aside.

7. In a medium-size saucepan or skillet, heat the oil over medium heat. Add the beef and stir-fry until no longer pink. Remove the meat. Add the potatoes, onions and carrots and cook for 2 minutes.

8. Add the water and cover the pan with a lid. Cook over medium-low heat for 5 minutes, or until the potatoes are almost tender. Add the meat back into the pot.

9. Pour the *shirataki* noodles into a strainer and rinse to remove any odor. Divide the noodles into 4 bundles and place them around the meat and vegetables. Add the soy sauce mixture and stir until incorporated.

10. Place the parchment paper directly on the food. Cook 3 minutes more, until the liquid begins to evaporate and the seasonings have been absorbed by the meat and vegetables.

11. Remove the paper and stir in the snow peas or green peas. Cover with the paper again to cook for 1 more minute. Discard the paper and serve hot.

Corn Rice Serves 4 Prep time: 10 mins (excludes rice)

INGREDIENTS

- 2 cups (400 g) cooked Japanese rice (see pages 26–27), hot
- 1 tablespoon butter
- ½ cup (80 g) fresh, canned or frozen corn kernels
- 1 teaspoon soy sauce
- Salt, to taste

METHOD

1 Put the hot white rice in a mixing bowl. Add the butter and soy sauce and mix until well combined.

2 Add the corn and gently fold it into the rice. Taste, and add a dash of salt if necessary.

Cabbage Salad
Serves 4 Prep time: 15 mins

INGREDIENTS

- ½ small Napa cabbage (about 1 lb / 500 g) or green cabbage, cored and coarsely chopped into 2-in (5-cm) pieces
- ½ teaspoon salt
- 2–3 clementines, or one 11-oz (340 g) canned mandarin orange slices, drained
- 2 teaspoons oil
- 2 teaspoons sugar
- Dash of pepper (optional)

METHOD

1 Place the cabbage in a bowl and sprinkle on the salt. Set aside for 10 minutes.

2 Scoop up handfuls of cabbage and squeeze out the water over the sink. Place in a clean bowl.

3 Peel and separate the clementine segments, and cut them in half. Add the fruit to the cabbage.

4 In a bowl, mix the oil, sugar and a dash of pepper (if using). Pour the mixture over the cabbage and fruit, and stir to coat.

School Lunches

List Foods of Each Color

Obento are fun lunches that children love to eat! In Japan, people try to include five colors: red, yellow, green, white and black. This promotes dietary variety and balanced nutrition. Seasonal foods are used as much as possible because they taste better and are fresh.

ACTIVITY

At the top of a sheet of paper, write out the colors Red, Yellow, Green, White and Black. Under each, write as many foods as you can think of that are that color. Then, mix and match when planning your next meal!

The concept, *me de taberu*, or "eat with your eyes," is also very important.

It suggests that we are more likely to eat well if the food is presented attractively.

Serving food in *bento* boxes or on smaller plates also helps with portion control.

CHAPTER 7

BENTO BOX LUNCH

お弁当

If you ever wanted a lunch that packed an eye-pleasing punch, look no further than *bento* lunches! The food in Japanese *bento* is not wrapped individually, but arranged attractively and packed tightly together. The confines of the box provide built-in portion control! If you don't have a *bento* box, you can use any suitable food-safe container with a tight-fitting lid. Look for cool picks to spear mini kabob ingredients and find fun vegetable cutters to make edible decorations that give your enjoyable, appetizing meal that finishing touch!

Here is an opportunity to put your Go! Grow! Glow! know-how to use. Make sure your *bento* meals include: foods of different colors (red, black, white, yellow and green); various foods in small portions; balanced nutrition (proteins, carbohydrates, vitamins and minerals); and a variety of tastes and textures.

While you're at it, be sure to follow these important safety rules: don't put hot food in the box; don't include raw fish; try to keep foods separated with a leaf or cupcake liner; and use condiments like ginger, soy sauce and vinegar to keep food safe to eat for longer periods.

In this chapter, we show you how to make tasty Super Spiral Sandos (sandwiches; page 108), protein-filled lunch box favorites like the Octopus-shaped Hot Dogs (page 103), slightly sweet Rolled Omelet (page 110) and more!

Kawaii Bento

Not only is the food *kawaii* (cute), but kids' *bento* boxes come in all sorts of cool shapes. This one looks like a Lego-style brick, packed with two layers of appealing healthy food—and it's a snap to put together. Make the cute rice balls or tuck in a sandwich, fruit and veggies. And don't forget to represent the 5 important colors!

Mini Mozzarella Balls with Soy Sauce and Grape Tomato Spears

When you marinate mini mozzarella balls in soy sauce, the little orbs absorb the sauce and take on a delicious flavor. Alternate them with grape tomatoes on a pick, and you've got another nutritious *okazu* (side dish) to fill out your *bento*. Hard cheeses are not suitable for this recipe.

Makes 4 skewers   **Prep time** 5 mins, plus 30 to marinate

INGREDIENTS

- 8 mini mozzarella balls (or mozzarella cut into bite-size cubes)
- 1 tablespoon soy sauce
- 4 grape (or cherry) tomatoes
- 4 long picks

METHOD

1. Place the mozzarella in a small bowl with a cover, or in a zip-top bag. Add the soy sauce to the cheese and close the cover over the bowl, or zip the bag closed.

2. Marinate the cheese in the refrigerator for 30 minutes to 1 hour. Don't leave it in for longer than this because the cheese will turn very brown.

3. Remove the mozzarella balls from the marinade and install 2 on each pick, with a tomato between them.

Soy-Brushed Corn on the Cob

TIP Another way to use a tasty marinated mozzarella ball is to tuck it into the middle of an *onigiri*!

Octopus-shaped Hot Dogs (see page 103)

Mini Mozzarella Balls

Kawaii Rice Ball (see page 30)

Soy-Brushed Corn on the Cob

Here's a tasty way to make use of corn-on-the-cob leftovers.

Makes 2–3 pieces   *Prep time* 5 minutes   *Cook time* 3 minutes

INGREDIENTS

- ½ ear cooked corn on the cob
- 1 teaspoon butter or oil
- 2 teaspoons soy sauce

METHOD

1. Cut the cooked corn into 2–3 pieces.
2. In a small skillet, add butter or oil and heat over medium heat for 30 seconds. Add the corn and roll it until coated.
3. Remove from the skillet and brush with soy sauce.

Corn and Ham Salad

This colorful side dish salad provides protein and carbs.

Makes about four ½-cup (75-g) servings   *Prep time* 10 mins

INGREDIENTS

- 1 cup (150 g) canned or frozen corn kernels, thawed
- 1¼-in (3-cm) thick slice of baked ham, diced
- 1¼-in (3-cm) thick slice of cheddar cheese, diced
- ½ green onion (scallion), trimmed, white and green parts, thinly sliced
- 2–3 tablespoons Kewpie mayonnaise, or other brand

METHOD

1. Place the corn in a bowl. Add the diced ham and cheese.
2. Add the green onion slices to the bowl.
3. Add the mayonnaise. Mix well.
4. If using for a *bento* box, place an individual salad portion into a cupcake liner.

Bento Box Lunch   101

Quick Lemony Cucumber Pickles
(Asazuke)

Pickles accompany just about every Japanese meal. They are crunchy and aid in the digestion of your food. Many pickles can take days or months before you can enjoy them. But these crunchy green cukes are ready almost immediately. The skin is left on, so it is important to get a cucumber with edible skin like mini or Persian cucumbers, or the larger English cucumber. Lemon juice adds a citrusy flavor that is perfectly paired with a dash of soy sauce.

Makes about ½ cup (75 g)
Prep time 10 minutes

INGREDIENTS

- 1 mini or Persian cucumber, or ¼ English cucumber
- ¼ teaspoon kosher salt or sea salt
- ½–1 teaspoon freshly squeezed lemon juice (from a ⅛ wedge of lemon)
- 1 teaspoon soy sauce

METHOD

1 Wash the cucumber and cut it into ½-in (1.25-cm) slices. Place them in a medium bowl. Add the salt and mix it into the cucumber slices. Let them sit for about 10 minutes.

2 Drain the water from the bowl and squeeze the water from the cucumber slices. Place them back in a bowl.

3 Add the lemon juice and soy sauce to the cucumbers and mix well.

4 Place 3–5 slices of cucumber in a cupcake liner to add to your *bento* box. This will keep the liquid from coming into contact with other food.

102 Chapter 7

Octopus-shaped Hot Dogs

Hot dogs or mini hot dogs cut into the shape of an octopus are designed to delight. Make cuts for 4 or 8 legs below the body and place into boiling water. Watch the legs curl up, just like an octopus!

Makes 1 serving   **Prep time** 5 minutes   **Cook time** 5 minutes

INGREDIENTS

- 3 mini hot dogs (cocktail franks), or 1 regular-size hot dog cut across the short dimension
- Ketchup, for dipping (optional)

METHOD

TO CUT

❶ For mini hot dogs: cut just below the tip (head) straight to the bottom lengthwise. Rotate 90 degrees and make another lengthwise cut through the halves to make 4 arms. You can stop here, or carefully cut each arm in half lengthwise to make 8 arms.

❷ For a regular-size hot dog: Cut it in half (cross-wise) first. Then, follow the directions listed above for making the arms. (Use both halves to make 2 octopuses!)

TO COOK

❶ Fill a saucepan with water. Bring the water to a boil. Add the prepared hot dogs. Cook for 1 or 2 minutes, or until the arms curl. Alternatively, stir-fry in a skillet with a little oil.

❷ Remove the "octopuses" with a slotted spoon. To eat, dip them into ketchup, if using.

INTERESTING FACT
Do you know what you call a group of octopuses? A consortium!

Bento Box Lunch

JFC! Japanese Fried Chicken (Karaage)

Japanese fried chicken is the most popular food for *bento*. It is made with moist, dark-meat chicken thighs. It tastes great either hot or cold. We shallow fry the chicken to use less oil when cooking. You can even make this recipe in an air fryer. Tofu is a popular substitute for chicken, however the tofu must be drained well (see opposite). Ask for an adult's help when frying.

Makes 2 servings   **Prep time** 10 minutes, plus 15 minutes to marinate   **Cook time** 10–12 minutes

INGREDIENTS

- ½ lb (250 g) skinless, boneless chicken thighs (about 3), cut into 2-in (5-cm) pieces, or ½ block (6 oz / 175 g) firm tofu, drained
- 2 cloves garlic, minced
- 3 thin slices fresh ginger, peeled and finely chopped
- 2 teaspoons soy sauce
- ½ cup (60 g) cornstarch or potato starch (*katakuriko*)
- ½ cup (125 ml) canola oil, divided
- Salt, to taste
- Lemon wedges, for serving

METHOD

❶ Set a cooling rack on a plate.

❷ Place the chicken in a bowl and add the garlic, ginger and soy sauce. Mix well. Cover and marinate in the refrigerator for 15–30 minutes. (If using tofu, cut the tofu into 3 slices. Cut each slice into 4 pieces for a total of 12 cubes, and follow the directions to marinate, using 1 teaspoon of soy sauce instead of 2).

❸ Place the cornstarch (or potato starch) on a plate. Roll half of the chicken or tofu pieces in the cornstarch.

❹ Heat half of the oil in a medium-size skillet over medium heat for about 30 seconds, until the oil starts to shimmer.

❺ Using tongs, add the coated chicken or tofu pieces to the oil. Be careful not to let the oil splatter! Cook for about 3 minutes, until the chicken starts to turn golden brown.

❻ Turn each piece. Cook an additional 2–3 minutes. Turn one more time and cook for another minute. Fry tofu pieces on all sides. For chicken, cut into one piece to make sure it is no longer pink inside. You may need to cook longer. With your tongs, place each piece of fried chicken or tofu on the wire rack.

❼ Add some or all of the remaining oil, if necessary. Repeat, coating and frying the remaining chicken or tofu. Sprinkle on a little salt. Serve hot or cold with lemon wedges.

How to Drain Tofu

Tofu contains a large amount of water. To make it crispy when frying, it is important to remove as much water as possible. Here's how!

METHOD

❶ Wrap the tofu in 2 layers of paper towels.

❷ Set the tofu on a plate. Place a slightly larger plate or small cutting board for a weight on top. Set aside for 30 minutes.

❸ Remove the weight and discard the wet paper towels.

❹ Pat dry with a paper or kitchen towel. Then, cut into pieces and follow the instructions to season and fry.

Rice with Tricolored Toppings
(Sanshoku Gohan)

This tasty rice bowl is a snap to make and is great for a *bento* box or a single-serving bowl. All the ingredients, except for the rice, are cooked in one skillet: Cook. Wipe clean. Repeat! Start with green beans, then the seasoned ground beef, and finally the scrambled eggs. Its crumbly texture, sweet and salty flavors and bright toppings make it a great meal-in-one-dish, and a favorite among young kids. You can substitute ground chicken, turkey or crumbled firm tofu instead of the beef. And you can always make the portion size smaller, for smaller appetites.

Makes about 2 individual bowls **Prep time** 15 minutes **Cook time** 20 minutes (excludes making the rice)

INGREDIENTS

FOR THE GREEN BEANS
- ¼ lb (100 g) fresh or frozen green beans
- ¼ teaspoon salt

FOR THE GROUND BEEF (OR CHICKEN, TURKEY OR TOFU)
- 1 tablespoon oil
- ½ lb (250 g) ground beef, ground chicken, ground turkey or crumbled tofu
- 1 teaspoon sugar
- 1½ tablespoons soy sauce
- 1 tablespoon mirin
- 2 tablespoons water

FOR THE SCRAMBLED EGGS
- 2 eggs
- 1 teaspoon sugar
- ¼ teaspoon salt
- 1 tablespoon water
- 2 teaspoons oil
- 2 cups cooked Japanese rice (see pages 26–27)

METHOD

GREEN BEANS

❶ Wash the green beans. Trim the stems. Cut each bean into 3 pieces on the diagonal.

❷ Fill a medium skillet with 2 inches (5 cm) of water and the salt. Bring to a boil. Add the green beans and cook for about 3 minutes. Drain the vegetables in a strainer. They should be bright green. Wipe out the skillet with a paper towel.

GROUND BEEF (OR CHICKEN, TURKEY OR TOFU)

❶ Heat the oil over medium heat for 30 seconds. Add the ground beef (or chicken, turkey or tofu) and stir-fry for three minutes, or until it loses its pink color.

❷ Sprinkle the sugar over the meat and stir-fry for another minute. Add the soy sauce, *mirin* and water, and continue cooking for about 2–3 more minutes. Transfer the meat and cooking juices to a bowl. Wipe out the skillet with a paper towel.

SCRAMBLED EGGS

1️⃣ In a bowl, beat the eggs, sugar, salt and water. Heat the oil in the skillet over medium heat for 30 seconds.

2️⃣ Pour the egg mixture into the skillet and scramble it with chopsticks for about 2 minutes. This makes very small clumps. Transfer the eggs to a bowl.

TO ASSEMBLE

1️⃣ Divide half of the rice into a bowl or *bento* box, filling it up about two thirds of the way.

2️⃣ Arrange half of the meat on top of the rice to the left. Next to the meat, add half of the green beans in the middle. And on the right, add half of the scrambled eggs. Spoon some of the leftover meat-cooking juices overtop of the meat.

3️⃣ If you like, garnish the tops of the portions in the bowl or *bento* box with vegetable cutouts (see pages 70–71).

4️⃣ Serve with a spoon.

Super Spiral Sando

It's not all rice! Bread is eaten every day in Japan, from delicious thick slices of toast to layers of colorful sandwich fillings all decked out in a rainbow row. *Sando* is the nickname for "sandwich" in Japanese. Rolled like sushi and cut into bite-size slices, this eye-popping sando is fun to make. Make it the night before, and then wrap and slice it in the morning. Make them for your lunch or a cool party platter. Vary the fillings with slices of chicken, turkey, egg salad and smoked salmon.

Makes 1 log—4–5 pieces   **Prep time** 25 minutes, plus 1 hour to chill

INGREDIENTS

- 3 slices soft white or whole wheat bread
- 1 tablespoon softened butter, or cream cheese
- ½ tablespoon mayonnaise
- 1 slice lunch meat of your choice (ham, turkey, chicken, etc.)
- 1 slice yellow cheese (for color: American or cheddar)
- 1 mini cucumber, cut lengthwise into 3–4 strips

TIP
Save the crusts and dip in egg to make a mini French toast sticks! *Mottainai!*

METHOD

1. Lay out a 10-in (25-cm) long piece of plastic wrap.

2. Place the 3 slices of bread in a vertical line. With a rolling pin, lightly flatten the slices.

3. Spread the butter or cream cheese lightly over the bread.

4. Take the piece of bread closest to you and lift it so the top of it is now slightly overlapping the second piece of bread. Press the seam down with your fingers. The spread topping acts like glue!

5. Overlap that strip just over the bottom edge of the piece of bread farthest from you and press down. You now have a single strip of bread composed of 3 segments.

6. Spread the mayonnaise over the whole surface of the bread strip.

7. Place a cold-cut slice on the segment of bread closest to you. Place a piece of cheese overlapping half of the cold-cut slice.

8. Place the cucumber strips horizontally about 2 in (5 cm) from the bottom, on top of the cold-cut slice.

9. Lift the bottom edge of the bread over the cucumbers and roll the sandwich forward into a tight spiral.

10. Wrap the plastic wrap tightly around the spiral to hold it together. Twist the ends. Place in the refrigerator for about an hour to overnight.

11. Keep the plastic wrap on and cut the roll into slices. Remove the plastic and tuck the slices into your *bento* box.

Bento Box Lunch 109

Rolled Omelet (Tamagoyaki)

This bright yellow omelet is slightly sweet, a bit salty, and adds several protein-packed morsels to this healthy lunch. You can add shredded veggies, zesty chives or green onions for more color and flavor. It is so much fun to roll the omelet, and then build the layers and roll it into the finished "log." It helps to have a non-stick skillet.

Makes 1 roll—approximately 6–8 pieces   **Prep time:** 5 minutes   **Cook time** 10 minutes

INGREDIENTS

- 3 large eggs
- 2 tablespoons water
- 2 teaspoons sugar
- ½ teaspoon soy sauce
- 1 tablespoon oil

METHOD

❶ In a bowl, whisk together the eggs, water, sugar and soy sauce.

❷ Add the oil to an 8- or 10-in (20- or 25-cm) skillet. Wipe the oil all around with a paper towel, sopping up excess oil. Save the oily paper towel! Heat the pan on medium-low heat for about 30 seconds.

How to make a Rolled Omelet

METHOD

❶ Pour about half of the egg mixture into the pan. Tilt it to spread the egg mixture around the sides.

❷ When the egg is set, about 1 minute, roll the egg to one side using a spatula. Wipe the open area of the pan with the oiled paper towel.

❸ Pour the remaining egg mixture into the pan. Lift the rolled portion up and let the egg mixture seep underneath it.

❹ When the egg is set, about 1 minute, roll the egg to other side of the pan using a spatula.

❺ Slip the rolled egg onto a cutting board and let it rest for 10 minutes before cutting.

❻ Cut the roll into 6–8 pieces.

Sugar Detective!

Let's play sugar detective! Now that you've learned how to read a nutrition label, use that knowledge to stay on the lookout for healthier options when it comes to sweets. Pick foods and drinks that have the least amount of added sugar, but also consider having smaller portion sizes and avoiding sugary treats before meals or bedtime.

SUGAR

How much sugar should you safely consume? To stay healthy, limit your sugar intake to 25 g or less per day, which is about 6 teaspoons, or 2 tablespoons.

FIND THE SWEET SPOT

Nutrition Facts
Serving Size 8 fl. oz. (240ml)
Servings Per Container 8

Amount Per Serving	
Calories 113	Calories from fat 0
	% Daily Value*
Total Fat 0g	0%
Saturated Fat 0g	0%
Trans Fat 0g	
Cholesterol 0mg	0%
Sodium 1mg	0%
Total Carbohydrates 30g	11%
Dietary Fiber 0g	0%
Sugars 27g	
Protein 0g	0%
Vitamin A 0% • Vitamin C 0%	
Calcium 0% • Iron 26%	

*Percent Daily Values are based in a 2,000 calorie diet.

INGREDIENTS: WATER, HIGH FRUCTOSE CORN SYRUP, GRAPE JUICE FROM CONCENTRATE, CITRIC ACID, NATURAL AND ARTIFICIAL FLAVOR, SODIUM CITRATE, FD&C RED #40, BLUE #1, POTASSIUM SORBATE.

GUESS
How many teaspoons of sugar are in this drink?

ANSWER
Over 6 teaspoons of sugar!

CHAPTER 8

DESSERTS & DRINKS

デザート＆飲み物

Desserts are big in Japan, but they are also small—that is, desserts are hugely popular, but the portions are smaller than what some of us are used to. They are made with some interesting ingredients, like *azuki* beans, which are rich in a protein. The sweet beans top our favorite fruit parfait (page 118), and are mixed with some sugar to make *anko* paste, an ingredient that is stuffed into the mini pancake sandwich, *dorayaki* (page 114).

Green tea is a popular drink in Japan. Among its special qualities are compounds thought to help prevent disease and boost immunity. Green tea does have caffeine, but our recipes call for very small amounts in the form of *matcha* (powdered green tea). *Matcha* is used in the tea ceremony in Japan, but is also used as a flavoring added to cakes, ice creams and drinks. Whisk up a warm Matcha Latte sweetened with a bit of honey (page 122), or add it to the batter of the Japanese Matcha Tea Cakes with Chocolate Swirls (page 116).

The key to enjoying sweets sensibly is to use wholesome ingredients, reduce the portion size and eat them at the right time of day!

TIP
Here are ways to enjoy *anko*—sweet bean jam!

- Make a spread of 4 tablespoons soft, unsalted butter with 2–3 tablespoons of anko. Keep refrigerated. Use to spread on toast for breakfast.
- Top vanilla ice cream with a spoonful of anko.
- Add it as a filling for cupcakes.

Sweet Pancake Sandwiches with Azuki Bean Jam and Strawberries (Dorayaki)

Dorayaki is a Japanese dessert (*wagashi*). It's a pancake sandwich made with sweetened *azuki* bean jam (*anko*), which is available at Asian groceries or online. *Azuki* beans are high in protein and fiber, and are used in many Japanese sweets. This recipe is from Kyoto *wagashi* maker, Aoi Tsuchida. The famous manga robot cat, Doraemon, loves *dorayaki!*

Makes about 8–10 2-in (5-cm) pancakes / 4–5 whole *dorayaki* sandwiches
Prep time: 15 minutes   **Cook time:** 10 minutes

INGREDIENTS

- 5 tablespoons flour
- ½ teaspoon baking powder
- 1 large egg
- 3 tablespoons sugar
- 1 teaspoon honey
- 1–2 tablespoons water
- 1 tablespoon oil
- 5–8 tablespoons anko (red bean paste – chunky or smooth) or jam
- 4 strawberries cut into 4 slices each (optional)

METHOD

1. Combine the flour and baking powder in a large bowl.

2. In another bowl, combine the egg, sugar and honey. Mix thoroughly with a whisk.

3. Add the flour mixture to the egg mixture and whisk them together. Add 1 tablespoon of water. Mix well. If the batter is too thick, add another tablespoon of water.

4. Add the oil to a large non-stick skillet. Spread with a paper towel. Keep the paper towel—you'll use it to keep the pan greased. Heat the pan over medium heat for about 1 minute.

5. Spoon batter into a 2-in (5-cm) circle. Repeat until you have 5 pancakes. Turn the pancakes over when bubbles appear. Cook for an additional minute, until the bottom starts to brown.

6. Place on a plate and cover with a kitchen towel. Repeat with the remaining batter.

7. Spread about 1 tablespoon of the *anko* onto a pancake. Place 2 strawberry slices (if using) on the bean jam. Spread a little more bean jam on another pancake and set it on top of the first pancake. Serve warm. Refrigerate leftovers, but *dorayaki* is best eaten the same day you make it!

Desserts & Drinks

Japanese Matcha Tea Cake with Chocolate Swirls

Who doesn't love a piece of cake? This cake mixes the slightly bitter taste of green tea with the sweetness of chocolate. Chocolate and matcha are great partners. Enjoy this dessert by cutting smaller portion sizes to help reduce the amount of sugar you consume.

Makes one 8-in (20-cm) square cake   **Prep time:** 20 minutes   **Cook time:** 25 minutes

INGREDIENTS

FOR THE CAKE
- 1½ cups (180 g) flour
- ¼ teaspoon salt
- 2 teaspoons baking powder
- 1 tablespoon matcha powder
- 1 egg
- ¾ cup (150 g) sugar
- 3 tablespoons oil, plus more to grease the pan
- ½ cup (125 ml) milk
- ½ cup (125 ml) whole milk yogurt

FOR THE CHOCOLATE SWIRL TOPPING
- ½ cup (95 g) chocolate chips

METHOD

① Pre-heat the oven to 350°F (175°C).

② Lightly grease an 8-in (20-cm) square pan.

③ In a mixing bowl, add the flour, salt and baking powder.

④ Place the *matcha* in a small mesh tea strainer. With a spoon, stir the matcha through the strainer into the dry ingredients. Whisk until combined.

⑤ In a separate bowl, add the egg, sugar, oil, milk and yogurt. Whisk until combined.

⑥ Add the wet ingredients to the dry mixture and mix until the batter is smooth and has an even green color.

⑦ Pour the batter into the prepared pan. Tap the pan on a table to get rid of the air bubbles.

⑧ To melt the chocolate: fill a small saucepan halfway with water and bring it to a boil over moderately high heat. Lower the heat to a simmer. Add the chocolate chips to a heat-proof bowl that's slightly wider than the saucepan. Set the bowl on top of the boiling water. Let the chips melt for about 1 minute. Stir with a spoon until completely melted.

⑨ Working quickly, drop the melted chocolate by spoonfuls evenly across the surface of the batter.

⑩ Draw the back of a knife or a toothpick through the chocolate in the cake batter in a swirl pattern. Place the pan on the middle rack in the oven. Bake for 20 minutes. Insert a toothpick into the center of the cake to check for doneness. If the toothpick comes out dry, the cake is ready. If sticky batter is clinging to it, continue to bake for 3 minutes and check again.

⑪ Place on a rack to cool. Slide a knife around the edge of the pan. Cut into 9–12 pieces.

116 Chapter 8

Desserts & Drinks 117

Japanese Fruit Parfait with Mochi Balls and Ice Cream (Anmitsu)

Anmitsu is a colorful fruit-mochi-and-ice-cream dessert with sweet red *azuki* beans and a drizzle of syrup on top. Crown it with a mini cookie or Pocky sticks to add a little crunch, and you have a real treat! With a variety of fruits, sweet beans and mochi made with tofu, this healthy dessert has protein, vitamins and fiber. To serve, group ingredients together for a lovely presentation.

Makes 4 servings   **Prep time:** 30 minutes   **Cook time:** 10 minutes

INGREDIENTS

FRUIT AND TOPPINGS

- 1 clementine, separated into segments, or 8–12 canned mandarin orange segments
- 1 kiwi, peeled and cut into half moons
- 8 strawberries, cut in half
- 1 firm banana, sliced on a diagonal
- ½ cup (approximately 100 g) sweet azuki beans
- ½ pint (250 ml) green tea or vanilla ice cream (optional)
- 8 chocolate Pocky sticks or small cookie wafers

FOR THE MINI MOCHI BALLS

Makes approx. 18 ½-in (1.25-cm) balls

- 1 cup (125 g) Japanese sweet rice flour (mochiko)
- 1 cup (150 g) soft tofu

METHOD

FRUIT AND TOPPINGS

Arrange the fruit on a plate for easy parfait assembly.

MINI MOCHI BALLS

1. Place the sweet rice flour in a bowl.
2. Add tofu by the spoonful and mix with two forks to combine.
3. With your hands, lightly knead until you've formed a soft dough.
4. Take about 1 tablespoon of dough and roll it into a small ball. Make a depression in the center of the ball with your thumb.
5. Continue forming mochi balls with the remaining dough.
6. Fill a bowl with cold water and ice cubes.
7. Bring a medium-size pot of water to a boil over moderately high heat. Add half of the mochi balls and cook them until they rise to the top. Gently swirl them around with a long-handled spoon. Lower the heat to medium-low and continue to cook for 1 more minute. With a slotted spoon, scoop them out of the water and place them into the bowl of ice water.
8. Repeat with the remaining mochi balls. Remove the mochi balls from the cold water and place them on a plate.

BROWN SUGAR SYRUP

Make your own syrup, or use store-bought maple syrup.

INGREDIENTS
- ½ cup (100 g) brown sugar
- ½ cup (125 ml) water

METHOD

❶ Combine the sugar and water in a small pan.

❷ Bring to a boil over medium heat. Take care, as the syrup will be very hot.

❸ Reduce the heat and simmer for 3–5 minutes, stirring occasionally, until the mixture thickens. Remove from the heat. The mixture will be thick, sticky and light brown. Put it in a small pitcher for easy pouring.

ASSEMBLE THE PARFAIT

❶ Arrange the fruit around the edges of 4 dessert bowls.

❷ Add a spoonful of *azuki* beans to the center of each bowl. Place a scoop of ice cream (if using) next to each dollop of beans.

❸ Add 4–5 mochi balls to each bowl, and then drizzle the Brown Sugar Syrup over the bowls.

❹ Add a few Pocky sticks or cookie wafers. Serve immediately.

Sweet and Salty Glazed Mochi Balls

Try these easy mochi balls (*dango*)—a popular street snack in Japan! They are made from short grain sweet rice flour called *mochiko* and soft tofu. Kaori Becker, mochi queen and author of *Mochi Magic*, kindly agreed to let us use her recipe. Tofu boosts the nutrition and keeps the mochi soft. Top with the sweet soy sauce glaze. Make the balls small, place them on a skewer and (carefully) chew, chew, chew.

NOT RECOMMENDED FOR CHILDREN UNDER 5

Makes about 24 balls   **Prep time:** 20 minutes   **Cook time:** 10 minutes

INGREDIENTS

- 1 cup (125 g) Japanese sweet rice flour (mochiko)
- 4 oz (100 g) soft or silken tofu, drained
- 1 tablespoon sugar
- Pinch of salt
- 8 wooden skewers or 20+ toothpicks

METHOD

1. Combine the sweet rice flour, tofu and sugar in a mixing bowl.

2. Gently mix the ingredients together with your hands, until you form a dough. It will feel like Play-Doh, or your earlobe, as described in Japan.

3. Form 1-in (2.5-cm) balls with your hands and set aside on a plate.

4. Fill a bowl with cold water and ice cubes.

5. Bring a medium-size pot of water to a boil over high heat.

6. Add half of the mochi balls. Reduce to medium heat. Cook until the balls rise to the surface (about 2 minutes). Cook for 2 minutes more.

7. Scoop out the balls with a slotted spoon and place them into the ice water bath. After a few minutes, remove the mochi balls from the cold water and place them on a plate.

8. Repeat steps 6 and 7 with the remaining mochi balls. Place 3 balls on each skewer, or 1 per toothpick. Set aside.

> This recipe was adapted from Kaori Becker's *Mochi Magic: 50 Traditional and Modern Recipes for the Japanese Treat*, Storey Publishing, 2020, with permission from the author.

SWEET AND SALTY SAUCE

This sticky sauce is the perfect companion to chewy mochi balls.

INGREDIENTS

- ½ cup (125 ml) water
- 2 tablespoons sugar
- 1 tablespoon soy sauce
- 1 tablespoon mirin
- 1 tablespoon cornstarch
- 2 tablespoons water

METHOD

❶ Sugar becomes extremely hot when turned into a liquid. Take care! Mix the ½ cup (125 ml) of water, sugar, soy sauce and *mirin* in a small saucepan and heat over medium heat until bubbles begin to form. Simmer for about 2 minutes.

❷ Mix the cornstarch and the 2 tablespoons of water together in a small bowl to make a slurry. Slowly pour this into the simmering sauce. Stir constantly. The sauce will thicken.

❸ Continue to cook and stir for another minute. Turn off the heat.

❹ Brush the glaze over the mochi balls. Let cool for two minutes before eating.

Desserts & Drinks

Matcha Latte

Matcha is roasted green tea leaves ground into a powder. It has a stunning green color and a slightly grassy flavor. Originally used for the Japanese tea ceremony, *matcha* is now also used for flavoring drinks, ice creams and cakes. Green tea is thought to have beneficial health qualities that are helpful in regulating blood pressure and fighting some diseases, among other benefits. *Matcha* does have caffeine, but we use it in small amounts. Check with an adult before using *matcha*.

Serves 1 **Prep time:** 5 minutes **Cook time:** 1–2 minutes

INGREDIENTS

- 1–2 teaspoons matcha (to your taste)
- 1 cup (250 ml) milk of your choice
- 1 teaspoon honey

METHOD

❶ Place the *matcha* in a large mug or glass.

❷ In a small saucepan over medium low heat, heat the milk and honey until bubbles begin to appear around the edges of the pan.

❸ With a wire whisk, carefully whisk the hot milk until frothy. Turn off the heat.

❹ Remove the pot from the stove. With a spoon, hold back the foam and pour some milk onto the *matcha*. Set the pan down. With a small whisk or spoon, mix the milk and *matcha* until thoroughly combined.

❺ Pour the rest of the milk and foam onto the *matcha*. Mix gently until combined.

Japanese Roasted Barley Tea (Mugicha)

Cha means tea in Japanese. In Japan, children start drinking small/diluted amounts of tea at a young age. You may be familiar with caffeinated green tea called *sencha*. *Mugicha*, a non-caffeinated tea made from roasted barley, is the most popular drink in the summer in Japan, and it is enjoyed by kids and adults alike! You can find it at Asian markets or online. It's easy to make and no sugar necessary!

Makes 4 cups **Prep time:** 2 mins, plus 2 hours to steep

INGREDIENTS
- 1 barley tea bag
- 4 cups (1 liter) water

METHOD
Fill a pitcher with water and add the bag. Put the pitcher in the refrigerator for about 2 hours. The water will turn a light brown. Throw away the bag. The tea is ready to drink!

Strawberry Soy Milk

There was a time in Japan when there weren't many desserts, so kids looked forward to strawberry milk with a touch of honey. This drink has lots of calcium and Vitamin D from milk, and Vitamin C from the strawberries!

Makes about 1½ cups (375 ml)—2 servings
Prep time: 5 minutes

INGREDIENTS
- 1 cup (250 ml) soy milk (or other milk of your choice)
- 1–2 tablespoons heavy cream (optional)
- 1 tablespoon honey
- 5–6 fresh or frozen strawberries, plus 2 whole strawberries, for decoration

METHOD

❶ Blend the soy milk, heavy cream (if using), the 5–6 strawberries and honey until smooth. Pour the mixture into 2 glasses.

❷ With the tip of a knife, starting from under the green stem, slice the remaining whole strawberries down the middle. This will split the strawberry, but keep it whole.

❸ Set a strawberry on the rim of each glass. Serve with a straw.

Desserts & Drinks

Resources

Many Japanese ingredients can be found in well-stocked local supermarkets. You can also find these ingredients at the following stores:

Japanese grocery store chains

At these markets, it will feel like you are shopping in Japan! Find fresh Asian vegetables, tofu and fish for sushi, and all kinds of staples and household goods.

- **Maruichi** (MA, CT, RI, NJ, VA) (maruichius.net)
- **Mitsuwa Marketplace** (CA, IL, NJ, HI, TX) (mitsuwa.com)
- **Nijiya** (CA, HI) (shop.nijiya.com) Online shopping is available too.
- **Tokyo Central** (CA, HI) (tokyocentral.com) Online shopping is available too.
- **Uwajimaya** (OR, WA) (uwajimaya.com)

Online shops for Japanese ingredients

- **Amazon** (amazon.com)
- **Dainobu E-Market** (dainobunyc.com) They have stores in New York too.
- **Gohan Market** (gohanmarket.com) They have a store in Georgia too.
- **The Rice Factory** (trf-ny.com) They have stores in New York and Los Angeles too.
- **Weee!** (sayweee.com/en)
- **Daiso** (daisous.com) A Japanese dollar store that has cooking utensils and other supplies. Check the website for locations throughout the United States.
- **HMart** (AZ, CA, GA, HI, IL, MA, MD, MI, NC, NJ, NY, PA, TX, VA) (hmart.com) A Korean supermarket chain with pan-Asian products that offers many Japanese food items.

Index

Allergies, A Word About 15
Aoi Tsuchida (Japanese dessert maker) 115
Aonori (seaweed flakes) 88
Apple juice 89
Apples 89
Azuki 16, 113, 115, 118–119
Bacon 88
Bamboo Shoots 72
Bananas 74, 118
Bean sprouts 82–83, 85
Beans 12
Beef
    Miso Ramen (ground beef) 84–85
    Nikujaga—Japanese style Beef and Veggie Stew (shaved steak or thinly sliced sirloin steak) 96
    Rice with Tricolored Toppings (ground beef) 106
    Shoyu (Soy Sauce) Ramen (sliced beef) 82
    Teriyaki Chicken Meatballs (ground beef) 80
Bell peppers 70, 30, 59, 88
Bento boxes 4, 6, 11, 58, 62, 70, 86, 98–111
Bonito Dashi 42
Bread 12, 57, 74–5, 108
Broccoli 11, 13, 67, 78–79,
Brown Sugar Syrup 119
Cabbage 11, 13, 46, 59, 77, 87–88, 90–91, 97
Cabbage Salad 97
Calcium 39, 123,
Carbohydrates 12, 99, 101
Carrot Ginger Dressing 73
Carrots 13, 22, 30, 58–59, 61, 65, 70, 72–73, 77, 87–88, 90–92, 96
Cheese 22–23, 34–35, 55, 57–58, 68, 70, 92–93, 100–101, 108
Cherry tomatoes 52–53, 68, 100
Chicken
    Chicken and Egg Rice Bowl (thighs) 36–37
    Japanese Savory Pancakes (shredded) 88
    JFC! Japanese Fried Chicken (thighs) 104–105
    Miso Ramen (ground) 84–85
    Pot Stickers (ground) 90
    Rice with Tricolored Toppings (ground) 106
    Super Spiral Sando (lunch meat) 108
    Teddy Bear Chicken and Veggie Omurice (thigh) 92
    Teriyaki Chicken Meatballs (ground) 80
Chicken and Egg Rice Bowls (*Oyako Donburi*) 36
Chili oil, spicy (*rayu*) 83–85
Chocolate chips 116
Chopstick rests (*hashioki*), how to make 40
Chopsticks 16, 18–19, 26, 40, 56, 83, 85, 95, 107
Chopsticks, building dexterity with 56
Chopsticks, cooking 18–19
Clementine Juice Jelly Cups 69, 79
Clementine peels, how to use 66

Clementines 66, 69, 74–75, 79, 97, 118
Condiments
    Easy Homemade Okonomiyaki Sauce 89
    Pot Sticker Dipping Sauce 90
    Teriyaki Sauce 60
Corn and Ham Salad 101
Corn kernels 30, 32, 44, 46, 80, 83, 85, 97, 101
Corn Potage 80
Corn Rice 97
Corn on the Cob 101
Counting to ten in Japanese 20
Crispy Soy Sauce Glazed Rice Balls (*Yaki Onigiri*) 33
Croquettes (fried patties) 62, 89
Crumbled tofu 84–85, 90, 106
Crunchy Edamame Rolls 57
Cucumber Coils 70
Cutting ingredients 22–23
Cutting terms 23
Daikon radish 42, 65, 73
Dark sesame oil 17, 28, 82
Dashi 14 39, 42, 61
Dashi Soup Stock 42
Desserts
    Japanese Fruit Parfait with Mochi Balls and Ice Cream 118
    Japanese Matcha Tea Cake with Chocolate Swirls 116
    Sweet and Salty Glazed Mochi Balls 120
    Sweet Pancake Sandwiches with Azuki Bean Jam and Strawberries 114
Dorayaki 115
Dried bonito fish flakes (*katsuobushi*) 42, 88
Drinks
    Japanese Roasted Barley Tea 123
    Matcha Latte 122
    Strawberry Soy Milk 123
    Yakult Drink 79
Easy Homemade Okonomiyaki Sauce 89
"Eat with your eyes" 9, 70, 98
Edamame Picks 71
Edamame 55–57, 71
Edible Decorations for Your Plate 70
Eggs
    Chicken and Egg Rice Bowl 36–37
    Japanese Savory Pancakes 88
    Miso Ramen 84
    Ramen Eggs—Soy Sauce Seasoned Boiled Eggs 83, 86
    Rice Sandwiches 34
    Rice with Tricolored Toppings 106
    Rolled Omelet 110
    Teddy Bear Chicken and Veggie Omurice 92
English cucumbers 50, 102
Equipment 18, 124
Five colors 11, 98–100
Fried chicken 104–105

Fruit
    Cabbage Salad 97
    Clementine Juice Jelly Cups 69
    Fruit Sandos 74
    Japanese Fruit Parfait with Mochi Balls and Ice Cream 118
    Strawberry Hearts 71
    Strawberry Soy Milk 123
    Sweet Pancake Sandwiches with Azuki Bean Jam and Strawberries 114
Fruit Sandos 74
Furikake 16–17, 28, 30–31, 43–44, 78
Furikake Popcorn 44
Garlic 80, 82, 85, 90–91, 104–105
Ginger 55, 62, 73, 77, 80, 82, 85, 90–91, 99, 104–105
Ginger, how to peel 73
Go! Grow! Glow! 12–13, 99
Gochisosama 9, 94–95
Gohan (Japanese rice) 26
Grape Tomato Hearts 68
Grape Tomatoes 68, 100
Grater 9, 23
Green beans 13, 67, 106–107
Green onions (scallions) 4, 34–37, 53, 61, 66, 72, 80, 83, 84–85, 87, 88–91, 101
Green onions, how to grow 66
Green peas 13, 30, 32, 58, 72, 92, 96
Green Veggies with Sesame Dressing 67
Gyoza wrappers 55, 57, 90–91
Ham, baked 34, 101
Hara hachibu ("eat until you are 80% full") 9
Heavy cream 123
Honey 59, 115, 122–123
Hot dogs 6, 77, 87, 99, 103
Ice cream, green tea or vanilla 114, 118–119,
Ichi-ju sansai ("1-1-3") 65
Inari (seasoned tofu pockets) 17, 58
Itadakimasu 9, 94–95
Japanese Fruit Parfait with Mochi Balls and Ice Cream (*Anmitsu*) 118
Japanese Matcha Tea Cake with Chocolate Swirls 116
Japanese rice, how to prepare 26
Japanese Roasted Barley Tea (*Mugicha*) 123
Japanese Savory Pancakes (*Okonomiyaki*) 88
Japanese Vegetable Fried Rice (*Chahan*) 72
Japanese-style Tuna Pasta 53
Japonica rice 16
Jello 69, 79
JFC! Japanese Fried Chicken (*Karaage*) 104
"Just One Cookbook" website 73
Kansha (gratitude) 94
Kaori Becker (author) 120
Kawaii (cute) 5–6, 19, 28, 30–32, 41, 58, 100, 113
Kawaii Bento 100
Kawaii Chick Onigiri 30
Kawaii Panda Onigiri 31
Kawaii Penguin Onigiri 32

Kawaii Rice Balls (*Onigiri*) 30
Ketchup Rice 78
Kewpie mayonnaise 14, 88, 101
Kid's Special Stir-fried Udon Noodles (*Yaki Udon*) 87
Kiwis 74, 118
Kombu (kelp) 17, 39, 42, 61
Kombu Dashi 42*f*
Kyushoku—Japanese School Lunches (*Kyushoku*) 96
Lemon juice 69, 78, 102
Lettuce 73
Lunch meat 108
Magnesium 39
Maki (sushi rolls) 18, 25, 50–51
Mandarin oranges 97, 118
Matcha Latte 122
Matcha powder 14, 113, 116, 122
Mayonnaise 14, 28, 34–35, 59, 77, 88–89, 101, 108
Me de taberu ("eat with your eyes") 9, 70, 98
Measuring spoons 18, 21
Measures, dry 21
Measures, liquid 21
Measuring 21
Measuring cup 18, 21, 27
Milk 122
Minerals 17, 39, 52, 99
Mini cucumbers 50, 52, 59, 70, 108
Mini hot dogs (cocktail franks) 6, 87, 103
Mini vegetable cutter 18–19, 22, 61, 70, 73, 99
Mirin 14, 86, 96, 106, 121, 33, 36–37, 46, 53, 60
Miso Dip with Vegetables 59
Miso paste 14, 33, 46, 55, 59, 61–62, 82, 84–85
Miso Ramen 84
Miso Soup with Vegetables 61
Mixing bowls 18
Mochi Balls 118–121
Mochi Magic (Storey Publishing) 120
Mochiko rice flour 16, 118, 120
Mottainai (avoiding waste) 10, 45, 66, 108
Mozzarella cheese balls 68, 100
Mushrooms 11, 46, 72
Namiko Hirasawa Chen (recipe developer) 73
Nikujaga—Japanese style Beef and Veggie Stew 96
Noodle-eating etiquette 83
Noodles
    Kid's Special Stir-fried Udon Noodles (*Yaki Udon*) 87
    Miso Ramen 84
    Nikujaga—Japanese style Beef and Veggie Stew 96
    Ramen 82
    Shoyu (Soy Sauce) Ramen 82
Nori (laver) 17, 28, 30–32, 34–35, 39, 43–45, 50, 53, 78, 82–83, 85, 92–93,
Nori Jam (*Tsukudani*) 45

Nori punch 18–19
Nutrition label, how to read 81
Octopus-shaped Hot Dogs 103
Okome (short- or medium-grain rice) 25–26
Okonomiyaki sauce 14, 87–89
Okosama Lunch— Kid's Lunch Special 78
Omelet 6, 35, 92–93, 110–111
Onigiri (rice balls) 4, 6, 17, 26, 28–33, 39, 45, 100
Onions 36–37, 46, 92, 96
Paddies, rice 25
Panko breadcrumbs 55, 62
Peppers, bell 70, 30, 59, 88
Persian cucumbers 34, 102
Pickles 65, 102
Picks, decorative 19, 68, 70–71, 99–100
Plums, pickled 28
Pocky 118
Popcorn 39, 43–44
Pork
    Corn and Ham Salad (baked ham) 101
    Japanese Savory Pancakes (baked ham or bacon) 88
    Kid's Special Stir-fried Udon Noodles (baked ham) 87
    Miso Ramen (ground) 84
    Pot Stickers (ground) 90
    Ramen (sliced) 82
    Rice Sandwiches (baked ham) 34
    Super Spiral Sando (lunch meat) 108
    Teddy Bear Chicken and Veggie Omurice (baked ham) 92
Portions, smart 12–13
Pot Stickers (*Gyoza*) 90
Potatoes 96
Protein 12, 16–17, 39, 55, 57, 65, 72, 82, 99, 101, 110, 113, 115, 118
Quick Lemony Cucumber Pickles (*Asazuke*) 102
Radish Balls 70
Ramen 82
Ramen Eggs—Soy Sauce Seasoned Boiled Eggs (*Ajitsuke Tamago*) 83, 86
Ramen noodles 82, 85, 87
Rice
    Chicken and Egg Rice Bowls 36
    Corn Rice 97
    Japanese Vegetable Fried Rice 72
    Kawaii Chick Onigiri 30
    Kawaii Panda Onigiri 31
    Kawaii Penguin Onigiri 32
    Kawaii Rice Balls 30–32
    Ketchup Rice 78
    Rice Sandwiches 34
    Rice-stuffed Tofu Pockets 58
    Rice with Tricolored Toppings 106
    Stovetop Rice 27
    Teddy Bear Chicken and Veggie Omurice 92
    Teriyaki Salmon Bowls 48
    Tuna and Cucumber Sushi Rolls 50
    Tuna Mayo Rice Balls 28

Wakame, Cucumber and Cherry Tomato Salad 52
Rice Balls (*Onigiri*) Three Ways 28–33
Rice bowls (*donburi*)
    Chicken and Egg Rice Bowls 36
    Salmon Teriyaki Bowls 48
Rice cooker 27
Rice Sandwiches (*Onigirazu*) 34
Rice vinegar 14, 25, 50, 52–53, 58, 73, 90
Rice with Tricolored Toppings (*Sanshoku Gohan*) 106
Rice-stuffed Tofu Pockets (*Inarizushi*) 58
Roasted sesame seeds (*iri goma*) 17, 67
Rolled Omelet (*Tamagoyaki*) 110
Safety, kitchen 7, 20, 99
Sake (rice wine) 17
Salads
    Cabbage Salad 97
    Carrot Ginger Dressing 73
    Corn and Ham Salad 101
    Wakame, Cucumber and Cherry Tomato Salad 52
Salmon and Vegetables in Miso Sauce (*Chan Chan Yaki*) 46
Sandwiches
    Fruit Sandos 74
    Rice Sandwiches 34
    Super Spiral Sando 108
    Sweet Pancake Sandwiches with Azuki Bean Jam and Strawberries 114
Saucepans 18
Seafood
    Japanese Savory Pancakes 88
    Japanese-style Tuna Pasta 53
    Salmon and Vegetables in Miso Sauce 46
    Teriyaki Salmon Bowls 48
    Tuna and Cucumber Sushi Rolls 50
Seasonal foods, eating 11, 65, 98
Seaweed 13, 17, 39, 42, 52, 61
Seaweed flakes (*aonori*) 88
Seaweed, roasted. See *Nori* (laver)
Sesame oil 59, 72, 85, 90
Sesame seeds 17, 43, 53, 67
Shiitake mushrooms 42, 46, 72
Shimeji (beech) mushrooms 46
Shirataki noodles 96
Shiso 16
Shoyu (Soy Sauce) Ramen 82
Shrimp 28, 65, 72, 88
Side dishes (*okazu*) 65, 67, 100
Silicone cups 19
Simple Nori Furikake—Tasty Seaweed Rice Sprinkles 43
Skillet 18
Snow pea pods 96
Soups and stews
    Corn Potage 80
    Dashi Soup Stock 42
    Miso Soup with Vegetables 61
    Miso Ramen 84

Nikujaga—Japanese style Beef and Veggie Stew 96
Ramen 82
Shoyu (Soy Sauce) Ramen 82
Soy milk 17, 62, 123
Soy sauce 14, 17, 28, 33, 36–37, 45–46, 50–53, 55, 60, 62, 67, 72, 78, 80, 82, 85–87, 90–92, 96–97, 99–102, 104–106, 111, 120–121
Soy-Brushed Corn on the Cob 101
Spaghetti 53
Spatulas 18
Spinach 82–83
Sprouts, bean 82–83, 85
Stale *nori*, how to refresh 43
Steak, shaved 96
Steamed Broccoli with Lemon Juice and Soy Sauce 78
Stovetop Rice 27
Strawberries 13, 71, 74, 115, 118, 123
Strawberry Hearts 71
Strawberry Soy Milk 123
Sugar Detective! 112
Sugar, determining the quantity of 112
Super Spiral Sando 108
Sushi 4, 14, 16–17, 25–26, 50–51, 58
"Sushi rice" 25–27
Sushi rolling mat 18
Sweet and Salty Glazed Mochi Balls 120
Sweet and Salty Sauce 121
Sweet bean jam (*anko*), enjoying 114
Sweet bean paste 16, 115
Sweet Pancake Sandwiches with Azuki Bean Jam and Strawberries (*Dorayaki*) 114
Table For Two USA 5–6
Tamari soy sauce 14, 55, 62
Tea 113, 116, 122–123
Techniques, basic 21–23
Teddy Bear Chicken and Veggie Omurice 92
Teriyaki Chicken Meatballs 80
Teriyaki Salmon Bowls 48
Teriyaki Sauce 60
Toasted sesame seeds 43, 53
Tofu
    Japanese Fruit Parfait with Mochi Balls and Ice Cream (soft) 118
    JFC! Japanese Fried Chicken (firm) 104
    Miso Ramen (firm) 84
    Miso Soup with Vegetables (soft or medium) 61
    Pot Stickers (firm) 90
    Rice with Tricolored Toppings (firm) 106
    Rice-stuffed Tofu Pockets (inari) 58
    Salmon and Vegetables in Miso Sauce (firm) 46
    Shoyu (Soy Sauce) Ramen 82
    Sweet and Salty Glazed Mochi Balls (soft) 120
    Tofu Croquettes (firm) 62
Tofu Croquettes 62
Tofu skins 17, 58

Tofu, freezing 62
Tofu, how to drain 105
Tomato Roses 71
Tomatoes 52–53, 68, 71, 100
Tongs 18–19
Tuna 28
Tuna and Cucumber Sushi Rolls (*Maki*) 50
Tuna Mayo Filling 28
Tuna Mayo Rice Balls 28
Tuna Mayo Rice Balls (*Onigiri*) 28–29, 50–51, 53
Turkey 85, 90, 106, 108
Udon noodles 14, 17, 87, 89
Utensils 18–19
Vegetable cutters 18–19, 22, 70, 99
Vegetable peelers 18, 20
Vegetarian options
    Dashi Soup Stock 42
    JFC! Japanese Fried Chicken 104
    Miso Soup with Vegetables 61
    Pot Stickers 90
    Ramen 82
    Rice with Tricolored Toppings 106
    Salmon and Vegetables in Miso Sauce 46
    Tofu Croquettes 62
Vitamin E 39, 52
Wa-Shokuiku ("Japanese food education") 4–7, 62, 80, 127
Wakame 17, 39, 82, 61
Wakame, Cucumber and Cherry Tomato Salad 52
Washing your hands 20, 36, 95
Waste, avoiding 10, 45, 66, 108
Whipped cream 74–75
Wonton wrappers 57
Yakult Drink 79
Yogurt 59, 79, 116
Yoko Ho (Wa-Sho Instructor) 80
Yukari 16
Zucchini 48

Acknowledgments

This book was produced with the support of Wa-Sho team members. We greatly appreciate special assistance from our Communications Planner & Designer, Sanae Uchinaka, Amy Fuentes, Nazumi Takeda, Miwako Felix, Chie Abe, registered dietitian and Christy Hirokawa. Yoko Ho and Yoko Saito were invaluable during the photography sessions. Illustrator Shun Yamaguchi has brought to life the "Elements of Japanese Cuisine." We also want to thank the US-Japan Foundation, JFC International/Nishiki, SMBC Global Foundation, Capitol Hill Community Foundation, JCCI NY/J.C.C. Fund, Zojirushi, Misuzu, ITOCHU, Japan Foundation, JCAW, Mishima, MUFG Bank, Q&B Foods, Mellam Foundation, Otafuku, Kikkoman Foundation, FNR Foundation, Juroku Cha and San-J for their continuing support. To our wonderful instructors who bring these recipes to students all over the country, *domo arigatou gozaimasu!* And to our dear families with love and gratitude.

A Note About the Photos

Food photography and styling was done in Debra's kitchen by our own Wa-Sho instructor and cookbook author, Yumi Komatsudaira, whose book, *Japanese Superfoods*, was published by Tuttle Publishing. She was assisted by her cheerful and very able son, Owen. Yumi also took several photographs of kids cooking. Father and son duo, Jacob Dylan Villaruz and Darwin Villaruz photographed the kids in action in Mayumi's kitchen.

    Shout out to Wa-Sho kids: Ria, Leo, Lincoln, Luna, Xavi, Kai, Aiko, Ada (who also drew the *kawaii onigiri!*), Lucien, Karin, Rina, Olivia, Tiffany, Lenon, Nina and Mia!

Published by Tuttle Publishing, an imprint of Periplus Editions (HK) Ltd.

www.tuttlepublishing.com

Copyright © 2025 TABLE FOR TWO USA

All rights reserved. No part of this publication may be reproduced or utilized in any form or by any means, electronic or mechanical, including photocopying, recording, or by any information storage and retrieval system, without prior written permission from the publisher.

ISBN 978-4-8053-1789-1

DISTRIBUTED BY
North America, Latin America & Europe
Tuttle Publishing
364 Innovation Drive
North Clarendon, VT 05759-9436 U.S.A.
Tel: (802) 773 8930 | Fax: (802) 773 6993
info@tuttlepublishing.com | www.tuttlepublishing.com

Japan
Tuttle Publishing
Yaekari Building 3rd Floor
5-4-12 Osaki
Shinagawa-ku
Tokyo 141-0032
Tel: (81) 3 5437 0171 | Fax: (81) 3 5437 0755
sales@tuttle.co.jp | www.tuttle.co.jp

Asia Pacific
Berkeley Books Pte. Ltd.
3 Kallang Sector #04-01
Singapore 349278
Tel: (65) 6741 2178 | Fax: (65) 6741 2179
inquiries@periplus.com.sg | www.tuttlepublishing.com

28 27 26 25
10 9 8 7 6 5 4 3 2 1

Printed in China   2505CM

TUTTLE PUBLISHING® is a registered trademark of Tuttle Publishing, a division of Periplus Editions (HK) Ltd.

"Books to Span the East and West"

Tuttle Publishing was founded in 1832 in the small New England town of Rutland, Vermont [USA]. Our core values remain as strong today as they were then—to publish best-in-class books which bring people together one page at a time. In 1948, we established a publishing outpost in Japan— and Tuttle is now a leader in publishing English-language books about the arts, languages and cultures of Asia. The world has become a much smaller place today and Asia's economic and cultural influence has grown. Yet the need for meaningful dialogue and information about this diverse region has never been greater. Over the past seven decades, Tuttle has published thousands of books on subjects ranging from martial arts and paper crafts to language learning and literature—and our talented authors, illustrators, designers and photographers have won many prestigious awards. We welcome you to explore the wealth of information available on Asia at **www.tuttlepublishing.com**.

Dreamstime photo credits: **Page 18 middle right** Bert Folsom. **Pages 82–85 outer margins** Hery Siswanto. **Page 92 bottom right corner** Ssstocker.

Shutterstock photo credits: **Page 18 middle left** WhitePlaid. **Page 18 second from middle left** Diana Taliun. **Page 18 third from middle left** OLIVER-stockphoto. **Page 18 third from middle right** MsMaria. **Page 18 second from middle right** Chachamp.